Homebuilding
& Renovating

Contemporary Homes III

320 PAGES ■ 370 COLOUR PHOTOS ■ 34 INSPIRATIONAL HOMES

Homebuilding & Renovating

Contemporary Homes III

This edition © 2016 Red Planet Publishing Ltd,
Original text and illustrations © 2008-2015 Ascent Publishing Ltd, St Giles House,
50 Poland Street, London W1F 7AX

ISBN: 978 1 9059 5990 7

All of the material in this book has previously appeared in Homebuilding & Renovating magazine - Britain's best selling monthly for self-builders and renovators (www.homebuilding.co.uk).

Design: Matt Milton
Managing Director: Mark Neeter

Printed in the Czech Republic by Finidr

For more information visit: www.thebuildingsite.com
email: info@redplanetzone.com
or call: 01480 891777

CONTENTS

CONTENTS

116

188   198

80   232

100

FOREWORD

For many years, modern design was anathema to the core British values of heritage and nostalgia. A sneaking suspicion of the contemporary as alien — perhaps picking up on its 20th century Internationalist origins — led homeowners, as well as planners and builders, to value the period home so much that we even try to build our new homes to look as if they are centuries old.

As this wonderful new edition of *Contemporary Homes* shows, however, things have changed. We now embrace the plurality of house design in the way we value it across all other aspects of our lives. This book showcases 34 of the best examples of the contemporary home in the UK. It will delight anyone who has an interest in how our homes are shaped and is a valuable inspiration for home extenders and remodellers — as well as those looking to build from scratch.

It is a triumph of ambition — these bespoke homes (featured originally in the pages of *Homebuilding & Renovating* magazine) are well beyond the comfort zones of the mainstream building industry. They require significantly more attention, detailing and of course investment than the mainstream new homes we see so often.

Yet they serve as an exciting glimpse into the future, with smart uses of internal spaces, plenty of light streaming into them and, perhaps best of all, a reinvention of the use of some of our most traditional building materials — brick, timber and stone.

'THESE BESPOKE HOMES ARE WELL BEYOND THE COMFORT ZONES OF THE MAINSTREAM BUILDING INDUSTRY'

Jason Orme

Editor, Homebuilding & Renovating magazine

The Package Reborn

A meeting of minds between a Cotswolds-based
architect and German package supplier has enabled
Robin and Miyuki Walden to build a unique timber
and steel-clad barn-style home

WORDS: DAISY JEFFERY PHOTOGRAPHY: SIMON MAXWELL

This home takes its cue from surrounding agricultural buildings, both in form and in cladding materials. Corten steel clads the front elevation, while Kebony timber, left untreated to weather to a silvery grey, and white render have been used to clad the rest of the house

As far as package builds go, Fox Furlong – the new barn-style home of Robin and Miyuki Walden in rural Gloucestershire – is quite different from anything that has been done previously. Traditionally associated with prioritising process over design quality, 'imported' packages have often struggled to gain credibility from both planners and the design community. Thanks, however, to the open-minded creatives at German supplier Hanse Haus, along with the vision of Cotswolds-based architect Renato Lusardi from Studio Lusardi, Robin and Miyuki have a striking Corten steel and timber-clad new home. It's sympathetic to its sensitive location too, taking the form of a contemporary barn.

"Our journey first began when we went to one of the Homebuilding & Renovating Shows, as we were interested in self-build after a friend of ours had done it. After moving up from London we were living in a farmhouse which was very exposed to the elements and was so cold and cost us a fortune in heating, which is why we wanted to look for something which was of high quality with low running costs," explains Miyuki. "I spent two years looking for a site for us and knew we also needed an outbuilding to be used as a workshop for Robin's ceramics business. After viewing another property in the village, the estate agent then showed us a Sixties bungalow and when we walked round the woodland site we were instantly charmed and made an offer."

Visiting the Homebuilding & Renovating Shows, the couple had the opportunity to speak with various package suppliers and immediately realised that this was the best build route for them, offering both a hands-off approach and an energy-efficient home that came with the added benefits of a quick build time and a fixed price. "I knew the kind of house I wanted and I didn't have the confidence that the UK companies were able to provide the same standard of house as the German manufacturers," says Miyuki. "The insulation levels, for instance, that Hanse Haus offers is significant; for me they were really incomparable."

Robin takes up the story: "The great advantage of the prefab system is that you are also much more aware of the final cost than you are with building the usual way. This was, for us, a massive plus. That's not to say there are no surprises, as when you

A 16 photovoltaic 3.8kW panel array has been installed on the south-facing pitched roof to generate electricity for the house

start to add extras on to match what you really want aesthetics-wise that's when you notice a sharp rise in costs. But being able to visually see what the price is from the outset means that you don't get hit with it later down the line."

"While Hanse Haus built the home, it was crucial we had our own architect as the planners insisted we respected the local Cotswolds style," says Robin. "We were fortunate enough to not only have an architect with vision, but one who understood both modern and urban homes, and who was also from the Cotswolds region and so knew the local vernacular. Our architect Renato got it spot on. Once he had done the sketches he sent these off to Hanse Haus who gave him the parameters to work within – he had to understand their system and work with what they were able to produce in their factory," explains Robin.

"The barn style really came about through Renato," continues Miyuki. "Given the location surrounded by traditional Cotswolds stone buildings, he suggested that an agricultural design would be favourable with the planners, which it was. We also didn't like the idea of having too much white render and he suggested using Corten steel to give a rustic effect, which works brilliantly. A friend of ours had also used Kebony cladding which we liked, and the zinc roof really finished it off – it also shows just how flexible Hanse Haus were as these aren't materials they tend to use."

Besides the kitchen and the staircase, the couple used Hanse Haus for pretty much everything. "We really wanted something magical in the hallway and so I looked for a specialist staircase designer who I found with M-Tech," says Miyuki. "I also wanted

to be able to run my cookery school from home and so needed to be able to specify a large, bespoke kitchen to house demonstrations."

In order to design a home that met their needs, early planning was key. "Luckily Miyuki is an expert in space management," says Robin. "All plans were drawn and she made cut-outs of our furniture to scale and moved them around the plans to work out where everything would go – even where the plug sockets needed to be!"

The interiors feel spacious thanks to open plan arrangements as well as voids in the hallway and in the kitchen – lifting the ceiling to create interest, while also providing a means of communication when the kids are calling downstairs to place their breakfast orders!

After flying out to visit the Hanse Haus factory in Germany to choose their fixtures and fittings, the house, in true prefab style, was built in the company's factory before being shipped over and erected on site. "The team on site were so responsive and reliable," says Robin. "The lorries arrived on 17 March 2013 and the roof was on within five days – we were moved in at the end of July. None of that would have been possible without the dedication showed by the five-man team. It's a method I really believe in and it's definitely one of the ways forward for building over here."

"We lived in the bungalow on site during the project to oversee everything," says Miyuki who acted as lead throughout the build, with Robin acting as "tea-boy" (his words!). "Living on site is such a good idea," he adds. "It was great to watch everything go up and to be there if anything was needed – although the team were so organised in knowing every detail of what they were doing I think they only asked us eight questions during the entire project!"

A separate guest annexe meanwhile was being built next-door at the same time as the house, and was designed by the same architect, although the couple instead chose a local builder to complete this element of the project.

Energy efficiency was a top priority for Robin and Miyuki, and the house has been packed with eco technology to keep costs down. A total of 16 photovoltaic panels line the south-facing roof, a borehole provides water, an air-source heat pump takes care of the home's heating and hot water, and a ventilation system keeps the temperature of the home constant. Underfloor heating throughout provides comfort against the wood flooring, while triple-glazed windows along with masses of insulation keep the home airtight.

"The ventilation system was a good investment, but then again you simply can't have a house like this without one as it would be too stuffy," explains Robin. "The borehole is also great and the thought of every tap in the house having our own water is wonderful – the difference in our energy bills has been significant.

"The house has come together even better than we'd imagined and the spaces work so well. The house was built in accordance with our needs and it's a real joy to live in."

The large open plan kitchen/dining/living area acts as a functional yet homely space. A floor-to-ceiling corner window at the far end overlooks the garden and wood. The kitchen was designed to house a large island (where up to eight people can be seated)

FACT FILE

Name: Robin and Miyuki Walden
Area: Gloucestershire
Build type: Barn-style self-build
Size: 200m²
Build date: Oct 2012–Jul 13
Land cost: £700,000
Build cost: £746,000
Cost/m²: £1445
House value: Unknown

CONTACTS

Package supplier Hanse Haus (hanse-haus.co.uk)
Architect Renato Lusardi 020 7684 7040)
Contractor Nathan Clarke (nathanclarkebuilders.co.uk)
Groundworks
P&P Groundworks (pandpgroundworks.co.uk)
Kitchen Das Küchen Studio (01784 438557)
Staircase M-Tech Engineering (mtechengineering.co.uk)
Landscaping Nick Williams-Ellis Design (01386 700883)

The homeowner's view

The spaces work so well – that's what's really magic about it. Because you're designing for yourself you're not having to compromise on space – all rooms have a purpose. In our old house we had a lot of wasted space, but not here. The only room we don't use everyday is the guest room. The house really works so well for us and having two teenagers, who get to have their own space too.

The house was designed to look over the wood, so the windows to the side make the most of this. The open plan kitchen, dining and sitting area is a huge success, which we all enjoy as the centre of our family life. The kitchen was designed to accommodate an island of a certain length so that it works perfectly for demonstrations for the cookery business, and it's a space that the whole family really live in and where we spend time together. The void in the ceiling (which is open to the first floor landing) works really well as it gives more light and an added sense of space. One tends to focus on the rooms but the wide landing upstairs and the spacious hall downstairs make a difference too.

We can't speak highly enough of the fast, efficient build and the high standards of the very detailed finish. The key to success with a project like this though is to take your time. You can't change your mind so you need to plan everything carefully at the beginning and don't rush it. If you're in a hurry then this is not the way to do it.

"All plans were drawn and we made cut-outs of our furniture to scale and moved them around the plans to work out where everything would go"

FLOORPLAN

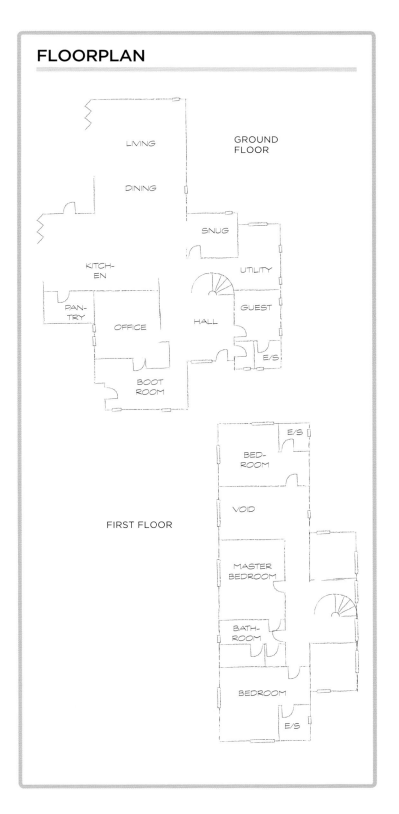

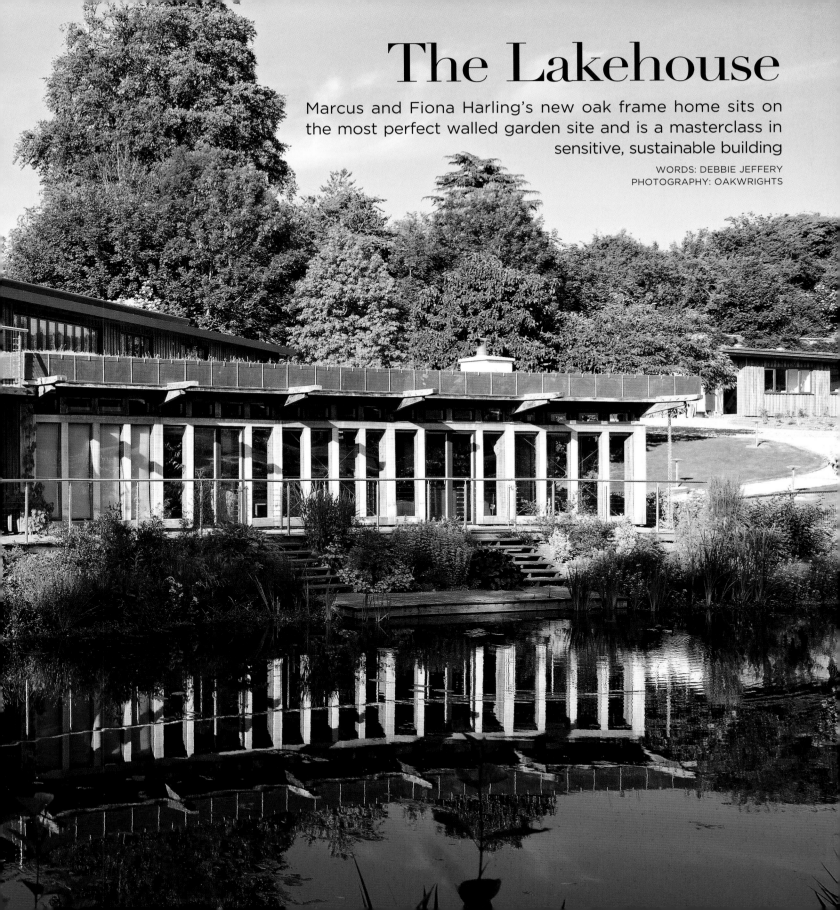

The Lakehouse

Marcus and Fiona Harling's new oak frame home sits on the most perfect walled garden site and is a masterclass in sensitive, sustainable building

WORDS: DEBBIE JEFFERY
PHOTOGRAPHY: OAKWRIGHTS

Designed to curve around the lake on a splendid walled garden site, the house features sedum roofing and larch cladding for an organic, natural appearance

Windows & Cladding
The blue-framed windows are from Velfac. Open joint vertical boarding is an unusual cladding style in the UK, being much more common in Scandinavia

Windows & Cladding
The blue-framed windows are from Velfac. Open joint vertical boarding is an unusual cladding style in the UK, being much more common in Scandinavia

Breakfast Room
The kitchen opens into a breakfast room with a woodburning stove, creating a sociable family space. French doors lead out to a sheltered decked area, perfect for informal eating and relaxing in the summer

What started out as a redesign and extension project for Marcus and Fiona Harling turned into a far more ambitious venture when the couple decided to replace a small Sixties bungalow with a brand new house. The Harlings had purchased the bungalow primarily because of its unique setting within a former kitchen garden to an 18th century Gothic Revival country house. A high brick and stone wall surrounds the 1.8 acre plot, and mature gardens incorporate a natural stream feeding two ponds.

"The bungalow was originally built by a couple who taught at an adjacent school, and our plan was always to completely remodel and enlarge the outdated building," explains Fiona. "We moved in and sought planning permission to extend the bungalow, which stood at the highest part of the site, but planning issues over scale made us rethink."

Marcus and Fiona decided that building a brand new house lower down on the site would give them all the space and light they needed. The couple drew up their own initial design for the house overlooking one of the ponds – aligning a faceted living room with the curve of the pond to make the most of the waterside setting. This helped to create the distinctive shape of the house, with large windows in the single storey living room, study and kitchen allowing ripples from the water to cast light inside the rooms and against the 18th century brick wall surrounding the site.

"Setting the house into the slope to decrease its external volume meant that a basement construction to the rear made sense," explains Marcus, a construction lawyer. In search of a high-performance solution, the couple looked at prefabricated systems and chose German supplier Kastell, who constructed the basement and slab.

With the inclusion of the basement and the contemporary design

Master Bedroom
The spacious master bedroom suite has its own private terrace enjoying views over the garden to the surrounding countryside. Clerestory windows bring further light into this room

this was always going to be a hybrid build, and an oak frame was an early aspiration. Finding an oak frame specialist with the right approach proved to be more of a challenge than the Harlings had expected, but after a false start with another supplier they contacted Oakwrights and were extremely impressed by the company's positive attitude.

"The Oakwrights team were instrumental in bringing all of our ideas together, and adapted their system to suit our contemporary design," says Marcus. "Chappell and Dix were our building contractors for the completion of the project, and picked up seamlessly after the frame was erected."

The house incorporates both passive and active eco features and has been orientated so that significant areas of glass face south, with the earth-sheltered rooms protected from the elements to the north. Insulation levels are high, and include a combination of natural cellulose insulation and sheeps wool, whilst exposed fair-faced concrete to internal walls and ceilings on the ground floor ensures that warmth is retained in winter and the interior remains cool in summer.

Externally, the walls and oak frame are clad with untreated Siberian larch, a resilient timber that weathers and will help to connect the building to the natural landscape. Green planted roofs over the sitting room and kitchen give added insulation and

"Our wood pellet boiler is very efficient and controllable. It's also much cheaper than oil, and we spent less than £500 on heating and hot water in the winter"

the sedum flowers also help to blend the house with the surrounding garden.

"A healthy environment was important, and material selection played a key part here," says Marcus, who project managed the build. "There are no fitted carpets to harbour dust – the ground floor is covered in natural linoleum and the first floor in engineered oak."

Underfloor heating is fuelled by a biomass boiler which uses sustainable wood pellets, fed automatically from a hopper – providing carbon neutral heating at a fraction of the cost of oil. In summer, hot water comes from an air-to-water heat pump which extracts warm, stale air from rooms, returning cooled air to provide air conditioning. A heat-recovery system is linked to the extract system which also has the ability to deliver filtered, cool, fresh air from the northern side of the building to the first floor.

The family carried on living in the bungalow on site during the protracted planning process and 20-month build. "It was quite a challenge, especially as Olivia, our third child, was born the week the piling contractors started on site," says Fiona. The couple and their children – Emily, 15, Jago, 11, and Olivia, now five – were excited to move from the old bungalow into their brand new home, which has exceeded everyone's expectations. "The house is almost part of the garden," says Marcus. "We feel extremely lucky to have found such a wonderful site."

"We're still on good terms with all the companies and contractors and there were no major stresses – despite this being our first build"

Marcus and Fiona designed their kitchen and had bespoke solid birch-ply carcasses and doors made to order and fitted with stainless steel worktops on top

The perfect site

The design of the new house has been heavily influenced by its setting in the Uley Conservation Area within the Cotswolds Area of Oustanding Natural Beauty, and securing planning consent presented a series of challenges which took time to resolve.

"Our initial idea had been to remodel and extend the Sixties bungalow on the site, but that was effectively restricted by the scale of an existing planning consent," says Marcus. "The key concern was external volume, so thinking laterally we developed 'plan B' – building a new house in a lower position on the site, adjacent to one of the large ponds at the centre of the original walled garden."

Sinking the rear of the ground floor into the slope running down from the brick boundary wall to the pond, allowed space to be maximised and meant that the Harlings could achieve a much larger house internally whilst still meeting the constraints on external volume.

Further twists and turns needed to be negotiated before planning consent was secured, however.

A detailed case officer report to the planning committee had initially recommended that planning consent should be granted, but when this was reviewed by a senior planning officer the conclusion was changed to recommend refusal. A very active and anxious period followed for the Harlings, who directly lobbied the planning committee and put together a strategy to form the basis of an appeal.

On the day of the planning committee meeting it was the house's numerous sustainable features which helped to ensure that consent was granted, despite the senior planning officer's recommendation. "We were told that the design actually contributes positively to the Conservation Area, which is good to hear when you're suggesting a contemporary design in a Cotswolds village," says Fiona.

FLOORPLAN

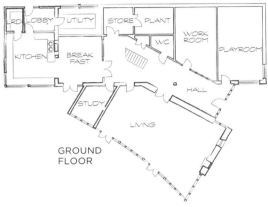

GROUND
FLOOR

FIRST FLOOR

A single storey living room, the study and kitchen all face south over the large pond. The two storey element of the new house includes five bedrooms, a breakfast room and playroom, which are joined to the living room by a large hall and stairway – one of the most distinctive features of the design. Positioning the store, plant room and utility within the basement area to the rear of the ground floor has maximised the available space whilst keeping the external volume within planning guidelines.

FACT FILE

Name: Marcus and Fiona Harling
Area: Gloucestershire
Build type: Self-build
Size: 435m²

Build Date: April 2085–Dec 06
Land cost: £685,000
Build Cost: £720,000
Cost/m²: £1,655
House value: £1.8m

CONTACTS

Oak frame Oakwrights (01432 353353)
Basement and slab Kastell (kastell-uk.com)
Building contractor, kitchen and bespoke furniture Chappell and Dix (01453 843504)
Groundworks D E Spencer & Sons (01453 822764)
Windows and external doors Velfac (01223 897100)
Internal doors Laidlaw (01902 600400)

Air-source heat pump Clyde Energy Solutions (01342 305550)
Wood pellet boiler Windhager UK (01249 446616)
Underfloor heating Jupiter (01276 859066)
Sedum roof Alumasc Exterior Building Products (01744 648400)
Linoleum Forbo Flooring Systems (0800 093 5258)
Engineered oak flooring Chauncey's (01179 713131)

"Looking out over the pond from the living room can be so restful, with the ripples from the water casting shadows against the walls and ceiling"

Beyond the Curve

Chris and Becky Taee have pushed the boundaries of house design and engineering to create a remarkable new family home

WORDS: JASON ORME   PHOTOGRAPHY: SIMON MAXWELL

Downley House is designed around two wings, separated by an extraordinary barrel-shaped centre, through which you can see the remains of the flint-clad, 19th century cottage that once occupied the site.

The 'Barrel' (right)
Lighting was a critical element to the success of the home. Chris and Becky chose John Cullen Lighting to provide a comprehensive design scheme

Staircase (above)
One of the many interior highlights is the dramatic glass staircase and balustrading feature, from Saxum

BEYOND THE CURVE

ownley House should really be the house they point to when looking for the ultimate example of what self-builders can achieve. From its conception – the moment Chris Taee and his wife Becky first discovered the isolated site in 2009 – to its eventual completion in April 2012, it has been an exercise in exacting specification, no-holds-barred design boldness and almost unbridled enthusiasm.

The site in question was one of three small properties that were tucked away at the end of a private track, a couple of miles from the nearest village in a peaceful hidden valley on the Hampshire/Sussex border. In the heart of the South Downs National Park, the Victorian flint-clad cottage had been under the same ownership since the Sixties with a long-term view to restoration. Unfortunately, shortly

after he started, the owner sadly passed away. It was then sold on to a local developer who demolished most of it, before Chris and Becky took a big leap of faith and bought a ruined wall and a large pile of rubble in 2009.

Despite being a very difficult place to get to, "it was the perfect spot for us – close to a great local school and very tranquil. I wanted to build our own house here, but I didn't know what I wanted to build," says Chris. So, as a man with considerable business management experience, he took a very professional approach. "We held an informal competition for six local architects (supplied by RIBA). Other than the outline room list, the brief was purposefully vague – a house that isn't obvious, that slowly reveals itself, using the best natural materials, and a prerequisite that it enhanced the landscape. And 'be brave.' I wanted them to push the boundaries on design.

Dining Hall
The glulam arches in the centrepiece 'foudre' section of the house have been treated with Fiddes wood oil to give them a white tint – and to avoid the dreaded orange glow

Exterior of the 'Foudre'
The cladding is a mix of wide and narrow pre-drilled oak boards – nailed on to battens using stainless steel nails and coach screws – over 100mm of foil-backed Kingspan Thermawall insulation, and a Tyvek rainscreen

The ultimate in wine rooms – not a cellar, as it's on the same floor as the kitchen – houses 1,400 bottles at controlled temperatures. The main living room (left) features warm oak flooring, a sandstone fireplace and interesting architectural touches, such as vertical windows

Kuche designed the kitchen, while the worktops are DuPont Zodiaq. As Chris couldn't quite figure out where to finish the glass splashbacks, he decided to cover the whole rear wall in glass, to stunning effect

The bedrooms are all designed with the idea of making the most of the private views across the valley. The windows are from Schüco

The master bedroom has an en suite, accessed by steps down to its slightly lower level; the bathroom features twin basins and Duravit sanitaryware

They all came up to the site to have a look, and went away to come up with something they felt would get them the job. The one that captivated us was Andrew Birds (from Birds Portchmouth Russum). His 10-page story book concept was unlike anything else." Becky was the one who said, "we have to step out of our comfort zone," and Andrew's design was the one that did that.

With six months of design development, what Chris and Becky got was a house that would reveal itself as you walked around it, making use of the topography and being both utterly modern and impressively natural. It comes in three parts – two living and bedroom wings (as well as the world's biggest plant room) separated by what looks like the top of a giant Conestoga wagon. It is, Chris says, in fact referred to as the 'foudre' – being French for a large wine barrel. Wine being one of Chris' great passions and a previous occupation (as a merchant rather than consumer), this is the undoubted attention-grabber of Andrew's design. "As well as being a spectacular space, it was an authentic homage to our love of wine on the part of the architects," says Chris. "And we both love it!"

So how does one go about building a 600m² home of almost impossibly bespoke design at the end of a very steep track in deepest Hampshire? "We managed it ourselves," begins Chris. "I took a couple of years off work and ran it as I would any other project, with me directing in collaboration with a very talented, hand-picked construction management team. With something like this, you need to eliminate risk as much as possible. So, without a main contractor, everything was done on subcontract packages, or agreed day rates. However, I needed to be here to make decisions daily. Everything was so bespoke and new to the people doing it, that it needed our attention all the time."

And if any house could claim to be at the cutting edge of house building, then this is it. The curved floor-to-ceiling arches in the foudre are glulam, but the main structure of the house is built from cross-laminated timber (often abbreviated to CLT) which is a form of engineered solid panel timber that is rapidly gaining a foothold in UK commercial building and multi-storey housing circles for its strength, airtightness and stability (Chris sourced theirs from Eurban, who imported it from Schilliger Holz in Switzerland). "Travelling to Switzerland to see it being built was a very inspiring moment for us," says Chris.

"During the build, we were living in a rented barn not too far away," continues Chris, "so the project for us was not terribly uncomfortable. I had a cabin on site which became an office with a great view for two years. As it was such an unusual and complicated build, it was critical to stay right on top of the program to maintain continuity and keep things really well organised."

Despite its size, part of the innovative approach to the house was to make it as energy efficient and airtight as possible. Chris specified two Awakdukt Thermo 'earth pipes' from Rehau – they work in a similar way to a ground-source heat pump, but use the latent heat in the ground to pre-heat (or cool) fresh air going into a mechanical ventilation heat-recovery unit. While they can reduce heat demand by up to 20 per cent, they are also really well served for cooling in the summer. There's also a 22kW ground-source heat pump running off three-phase electricity (which is used as an efficient way of delivering heavy loads) which supplies all the domestic hot water and the underfloor heating. The house has its own water supply courtesy of a 250-foot borehole. All of this kit is held in not just one but two plant rooms, connected by nine 150mm ducts – it is a very well thought-out engineering operation.

Inside as well as outside, the house is simply breathtaking. The old ruined wall provides a magical historical backdrop to the majestic scale and simplicity of the foudre, which is used as a grand dining hall, complete with a contemporary take on the minstrels' gallery idea. A hugely ambitious glazed landing and staircase structure links all three parts of the house at first floor level (the unfortunate glazing contractor had to re-supply all of the curved toughened glass that had been made incorrectly – not a good day at their offices, one assumes!).

The architect has incorporated generous 'buffer' areas between the living and circulation spaces and the bedrooms to allow an element of privacy within the open plan context. A 2.95m ceiling height adds to the sense of space, although at circa 600m² this was never going to feel like a poky house.

"There are two key things I've learned," says Chris. "You need to have an honest relationship with – as well as absolute faith in – your architect. And secondly, it is critical to be on site daily to achieve this level of bespoke detail." He has, undoubtedly, pushed the boundaries of design and house engineering, as well as displayed a tireless dedication to getting everything done absolutely right. To the outsider, looking at a house of this scale and quality is all a little bit overwhelming – but the result is hugely admirable.

FACT FILE

Name: Chris and Becky Taee
Area: Hampshire
Build type: Self-build
Size: 607m²
Build date: June 2010–Apr 12

Land cost: £685,000
Build cost: £2.5m
Cost/m²: £4,118
House value: £4.5m

CONTACTS

Architect Birds Portchmouth Russum (020 7253 8205
Heat pump NIBE (0845 095 1200)
Underfloor heating Nu-Heat (0800 731 1976)
Mechanical ventilation heat-recovery system Vent-Axia (0844 856 0590)
Earth pipes Rehau (rehau.com
Windows Schüco (01908 282111)
Wood treatment Fiddes & Sons (02920 340323)
Blanchon (blanchon.co.uk
Oak flooring Silvan (0116 239 5354)
Carpets Jacaranda (01536 762697)
External oak WL West (01798 861611)
Jurassic stone Lovell Purbeck (01929 439255)
Sandstone Lambs (01403 785141)
Masonry Guy Goodens (01730 821781)
Electrician Emery Power & Light (07980 834972)
Plumbing NJ Bryan Plumbing and Heating (02380 694231)
Ironmongery Ize Finishes

(ize.info)
Sinks Wharf Solid Surfaces (01730 812822)
Metalwork Artec Engineering (01243 375555)
External stairs Canal Engineering (0115 986 6321)
Copper roofing Peters Roofing (020 8655 3598)
Flat roofing Roofline (02392 232032)
Groundworks and landscaping PR Collins (07771 877840)
Tiles Royal Mosa (mosa.nl)
Wine room Sorrells (01268 570880)
Resin flooring Floortrak (01794 885996)
Decoration David Stanbrook (01962 881460)
Kitchen Kuche (0845 094 9591)
Garage door Rundum Meir (01512 806626)
Lighting design John Cullen Lighting (020 7371 5400)
Glass balustrading and stairs Saxum (01803 866893)
Fires Gazco & Stovax (stovax.com)
Lighting control system Cooper Controls (01923 495495)

FLOORPLAN

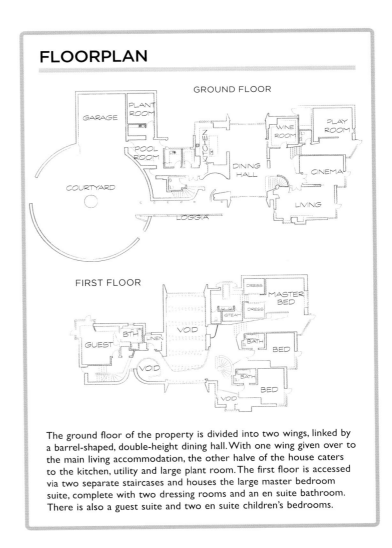

The ground floor of the property is divided into two wings, linked by a barrel-shaped, double-height dining hall. With one wing given over to the main living accommodation, the other halve of the house caters to the kitchen, utility and large plant room. The first floor is accessed via two separate staircases and houses the large master bedroom suite, complete with two dressing rooms and an en suite bathroom. There is also a guest suite and two en suite children's bedrooms.

Maximum Impact

Meticulous design and planning goes a long way when making the most of a tight urban site and budget – as Stephen and Cecilia Blowers' new home goes to show

WORDS: DEBBIE JEFFERY PHOTOGRAPHY: SIMON MAXWELL

If anyone ever asks me who my worst client has been, then the answer is simple – unfortunately, it would have to be me," admits architect Stephen Blowers. "Designing my own home has been the hardest job I've ever done. I created option after option – trying to bridge the gap between aspiration and budget – but always returned to the original courtyard concept I'd sketched out one night in a pub."

Stephen's concerns for the sloping brownfield site he'd purchased in 2008 were fully justified. The land had previously belonged to developer architects who failed to achieve planning permission for a variety of larger schemes. With such an unpromising planning history, the plot could have proved something of a white elephant, but Stephen was determined to build a contemporary house on a budget as restricted as the site itself.

Located at the end of a street of typical Thirties houses in London's East Dulwich, and bounded on three sides by neighbouring properties, the plot measures just 17.1 x 11.5metres – and was formed when part of a garden was combined with three ex-local authority garages.

"Unlike most architects, I hadn't really considered building my own house until this piece of land came up for auction next-door to my aunt's house," says Stephen. "In many ways I ended up building almost by accident."

Stephen, who is a partner at architectural practice Designcubed, fortunately went on to achieve planning permission for a modest single storey dwelling, and developed this to create a home akin to a Tardis. Built out to the perimeter walls, the exterior appears small and unassuming with few windows, but this modest façade belies the feeling of light, space and seclusion within.

Opaque windows maintain a feeling of privacy and security from the street, and an abundance of natural light is provided to the living spaces through two large rooflights. Wide windows and doors open on to two courtyards – positioned to the front and rear of the floorplan – which are key to the building's success.

Stephen married his Swedish partner Cecilia (who works for Designcubed as office manager) just before tenders for the construction of their new home came in. The first quote, which arrived on the day the couple departed for their honeymoon in France, was somewhat expected but well above what Stephen had hoped for and was completely out of reach of the budget. "It wasn't the best news we could have had," Stephen admits, "but in

The kitchen features inexpensive Ikea units which have been cleverly customised. A large island stands between the food preparation areas and the dining table, and is topped by an oak worktop. Two low-hung pendants compliment the oak flooring

the end there was a wide range of prices, and we chose the one which was significantly less than the other tenders. This should have perhaps alerted suspicion, but it was the only way we could afford to build this house so we didn't really have a choice."

Work finally began on the site in 2011, three years after Stephen first bought the land. But a handful of months in, the Blowers hit a major stumbling block. "Unfortunately, the builder we were using got into financial difficulties and left the site at short notice, just three months into the build," explains Stephen. "The result was that overnight I became a true self-builder and managed the rest of the project myself – employing a different builder and purchasing materials directly in order to keep things moving and to stay within budget." As the house began to take shape, Stephen tried to negotiate deals with suppliers, and purchased furniture on eBay in order to keep costs down. He and Cecilia moved into their partially completed house in May 2012, prioritising some of the key tasks and leaving others until more funds became available.

Despite the tight budget, the resulting build features a considered palette of materials. Outside, rich perimeter walls built in block and

clad in brick provide a vibrant counterpoint to the softer, mellowing western red cedar cladding and decking used in the courtyards. The flat roof, which ensures the house is low in profile, was formed from a liquid plastic membrane and rigid insulation on a plywood deck, supported on a web of composite engineered joists.

Inside, the beam and block floors have been finished with rigid insulation and screed, and topped in a mix of solid oak and porcelain tiles. The internal doors were imported from a factory in the tiny Swedish village where Cecilia grew up, the windows and wood flooring came from Denmark, and the kitchen units, fitted cupboards and wardrobes were all purchased from Ikea and have been adapted and customised for a bespoke look.

Space heating and hot water are provided by an air-source heat pump located in the entrance courtyard, and the infrastructure is in place to later connect solar thermal (hot water) panels and photovoltaics when funds allow. Large rooflights and extensive glazing also mean that artificial lighting is never needed during daylight hours in the main light-filled living spaces.

The difference in height (the living space is 0.5m lower than the kitchen) lends a feeling of volume to the living room. A partial wall acts as a room divider, as well as providing all-important storage and a discreet spot to mount the flatscreen TV

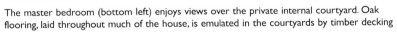
The master bedroom (bottom left) enjoys views over the private internal courtyard. Oak flooring, laid throughout much of the house, is emulated in the courtyards by timber decking

MAXIMUM IMPACT

The home was designed to maximise every inch of available space on this tight, urban plot — formerly home to three local authority-owned garages

"When the sun comes out it's magical as the light is constantly changing. You can literally watch the sun track throughout the day, rather like a sundial," Stephen says. "After spending 12 years living in a one-bed flat without any outdoor space, it's been a massive change to move into such a bright and open-plan home. Every day we feel spoilt by this house."

FACT FILE

Name: Steven and Cecilia Blowers
Area: London
Build type: Self-build
Size: 121m²

Build date: Aug 2011–May 12
Land cost: £140,000
Build cost: £230,000
Cost/m²: £1,901
House value: £875,000

CONTACTS

Architect Designcubed (07887 995595 design-cubed.co.uk)
Second builder Keith Elliott (07881 595750)
Structural engineer Malishev Wilson Engineers (020 7251 6638)
Composite aluminium and timber windows Velfac (01223 897100)
Folding sliding doors Express Bi-folding Doors (0800 121 4809)
Rooflights Glazing Vision (0333 8000 881)
Cedar cladding Vincent Timber (0121 772 5511)
Timber deck supply Round Wood of Mayfield (01435 867072)
Front gate and storage doors The Garden Trellis Company (01255 688361)
Decothane roof membrane Liquid Plastics (01772 259781)
Roof installation Athena Roofing (020 8640 7777)
Ecodan air-source heat pump Mitsubishi Electric (01707 282880)
Kinetic ventilation and heat recovery unit Vent-Axia (0844 856 0590)

Underfloor heating Polypipe (polypipe.com
Solid oak flooring Junckers (01376 534700)
Oak floor fitting Castledene Flooring (0844 225 0341)
Kitchen, wardrobes and storage Ikea (0845 358 3363)
Acrylic worktops Hanex (0845 603 7811)
Hanex and oak worktops Mr Worktops (020 7733 2882)
Lighting concept Hoare Lea Lighting (020 3668 7100)
Main light fixtures Cube Lighting (01442 876676)
Rooflight LED lights NJO Technology (01539 730093)
Pendant lights over kitchen island Original BTC (originalbtc. com)
Interior doors Dooria Doors (Sweden) (dooria.se_
Taps and showers Grohe (0871 200 3414)
Tiles Domus (020 8481 9500)
Sanitaryware Duravit (duravit. co.uk)
CP Hart (cphart.co.uk)
Bathroom shower screens and mirrors Bowalker Windows (0800 881 5640)

Making the most of a small plot

Stephen and Cecilia's new home has been partially cut into the slope of the compact site to maintain a level access and a low profile to the street. Brick perimeter walls are a key part of the design and make the most efficient use of the limited space available, without overlooking neighbouring houses or compromising on privacy.

Inside, the open plan layout creates a feeling of space, although a change in level from the kitchen/dining area down three steps to the sunken living area provides a degree of separation, too.

"I was also determined that the house should have three bedrooms to maximise its potential value, which meant that certain sacrifices had to be made – including Cecilia's request for a utility room and an entrance hall," says Stephen. "Instead of a corridor, I created an entrance courtyard with a large external store, and plenty more built-in storage throughout the house – including a cupboard to contain the washing machine and dryer."

Another unusual feature is the design of the master bathroom, which is separated from the main bedroom by a walk-through wardrobe/dressing room – creating a totally private suite in one corner of the house. "It's one of our favourite features, because there's a buffer between the bedroom and bathroom," says Stephen. "We currently use the third bedroom as an office, and the whole layout works fantastically well, particularly when we have guests as the house just seems to absorb them."

FLOORPLAN

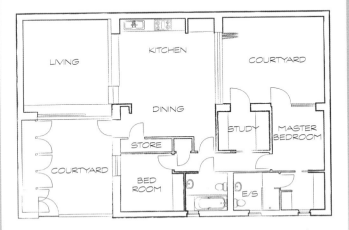

The living areas and bedroom accommodation have been arranged in two 'blocks' to provide a sense of separation in this single storey home, while two courtyards ensure that all the principal rooms are filled with natural light. In the open plan living space, a difference in ceiling height helps differentiate the kitchen and dining space from the living area. Opaque glass windows provide the bathrooms – located on the street-facing façade – with daylight without compromising privacy.

Modern Classic

Mike and Ann Urwin's beautiful new home is a masterclass in how contemporary shapes can, in fact, add to awe-inspiring natural surroundings

WORDS: JASON ORME
PHOTOGRAPHY: JOHN NEED

Steel, Glass and Stone
The new building sits in the garden of the couple's previous house and enjoys fantastic views. Built entirely out of steel frame, the strong structure connects to a barn/office building that was a condition of planning permission (granted as a croft). The building has a series of three cascading roofs – one flat, two sloping. Built out of a steel frame and supported by impressively lean steel pillars (see above)

Four steel posts support the steel-frame roof structure in the brilliant open-plan living and dining space. A Charnwood stove provides a focus but the views over Loch Awe are the real attraction. Variable-width pine boards accentuate the 5 deg slope

A series of angular roofs were employed to complement the natural contours of the land. Fernhill Stone (mostly the Southern Ledgestone range) was used: a very good 'cladding' designed to replicate the appearance of natural stone. The main large doors are from Sky-Frame, the rest are from NorDan; the timber is Siberian Larch

MODERN CLASSIC

If ever a house showed how contemporary design can not only fit well in to a country setting but also enhance it, it is this one. Designed for Mike and Ann Urwin – dentists who wanted a change of scene and pace for their retirement – this astonishingly beautiful home on the edge of the astonishingly beautiful Loch Awe (in the western Highlands) makes you wonder why everyone doesn't build like this.

"We lived in the house next door," begins Mike. "It was a large period home with all of the benefits, and problems, that older houses bring. We had a few requirements of a new house: We wanted to downsize but be able to accommodate our children and grandchildren; that it would be easier and cheaper to heat; to be as green as possible; and also important was that it enabled us to enjoy the beautiful views and the fantastic location."

"We had an open mind as to the style of the house," explains Ann. "We had always been interested in house design and we had the opportunity here to build something modern. We felt that it would have been odd to somehow build a new house in period style."

Mike and Ann had already identified a main contractor who they were very keen to work with and asked them to identify an architect. The result was that two firms – one local, one from Glasgow – were invited to visit the site and come up with some initial sketches.

"The site gained consent as a croft," begins the architect that won the informal competition, Alastair MacIntyre of McInnes Gardner (the Glasgow firm), "and as such had certain restrictions and conditions with it. Mike and Ann need to operate it as a live, working farm, and part of the brief was to create storage buildings/barns as well as the new house. But, that aside, given the isolated nature of the site, we could pretty much build in any style we wanted." There is a plethora of newly built or in-construction one-off homes in the area, from a baronial traditional new home to a Canadian-style log house, and more besides – all on beautiful sites and all with amazing views.

Steel posts support a pod-like structure which incorporates a first floor-study

"We were impressed with Alastair's approach and happy to pursue something quite modern. It seemed the natural approach to meet our brief," says Mike. "They were very encouraging of a modern scheme," confirms Alastair. "In many ways the site brought about the initial concepts for the design. The house sits at the top of a small valley, the slopes of which were used as inspiration for those amazing roof lines. Then, in simple terms, a large glass box sits on top of a suspended tray which provides a covered deck as well as the main living areas (allowing them to enjoy the views). The master bedroom and twin study areas are in this space too but are recessed back. Below the main deck, a series of guest bedrooms, all with en suites, are built into the semi-basement level."

It would have been all too easy for this to be another Modernist white box that looked like it had been dropped on to the site from Mars – something that Alastair was keen to avoid, despite the strong modern lines and bold roof structure. "We purposely chose materials that were more natural, enabling the house to be relatively 'camouflaged' in its setting. So there's glass, which is transparent, there's larch, stone and render which has been coloured in very neutral tones. It doesn't shout at all."

The undoubted triumph of this place, however, is the series of three cascading roofs – one flat, two sloping. Built out of a steel frame and supported by impressively lean steel pillars, it is a house that wears its engineering nous on its sleeve, and is all the better for it. The sloping monopitch roof over the main living area feels brilliantly heavy and is the focal point of the design, highlighted internally with pine boards cut to varied gauges. It's simple, all very mid-century, and hugely effective in allowing bags of light and air to circulate. Even better, just as you think with all this glass and steel that it could feel light and temporary, the whole thing is anchored to the ground with a chunky stone chimney and facing wall. "It's actually a stone cladding system, from Fernhill Stone," explains Alastair. "I must admit, when Mike and Ann told me that they wanted to use a stone cladding system rather than natural stone, my heart sank. But I had a good look at it and it looks very, very effective. Of course it saves considerably, particularly on labour, against natural stone, too." A garage and storage space – part of the crofting requirement – at the top of the site is cleverly linked to the main house with a covered porte-cochère. Again, all very mid-century.

Despite having never built anything like this before – or

anything using as much steel – the contractors did an exceptional job. "Good detailing and quantity of drawings is key," says Alastair. "The less you leave to the imagination, the less room there is for things to go wrong. The house required a lot of engineering design but once that had been done, all the builders had to do was follow the instructions." Alastair drove the couple of hours up from Glasgow every week or two to check in on the project's progress.

Another aspect that Mike and Ann are particularly happy with is the home's performance. "We chose a ground-source heat pump system, powered by PV (photovoltaic) panels, which feeds the underfloor heating and is complemented by a mechanical ventilation and heat recovery system," explains Mike. "Considering the winters up here, we've been very impressed by how warm the house is naturally – largely due to the huge levels of south-facing glazing.

"We couldn't be happier. Alastair has created an amazing home for us which has that hidden secret to it – being light, warm and airy, taking great advantage of our site while, at the same time, feeling like a warm, characterful family home," adds Mike.

"Designing a home with clients who were willing to embrace contemporary design on a site this perfect, with the views, was a unique opportunity – and one I'll probably never get again," admits Alastair. But, of course, the best homes are about so much more than good design. And when you start with a design as good as this, and mix in that feeling of 'home', you get something very special indeed. Ann's description of it as a "beautiful home in a field where we could quietly observe nature," is modesty in the extreme.

The roof construction

The crowning glory of the house is a large, gently sloping roof that almost appears to support the glass and steel structure below. "We wanted a light quality to the elevation overlooking the Loch, and a steel frame structure enabled us to support the roof as well as incorporate lots of glass without a hint of movement," says architect Alastair MacIntyre. Four steel posts hold up the roof on the loch side, while internally it rests on a masonry retaining wall – it's an awe-inspiring mix of design and clever engineering. The roof itself is a steel frame on to which plywood, rigid insulation and another layer of plywood is placed (a bit like a structural insulated panel system, without the structure) and finished off in a single ply membrane (it's a bit lighter than zinc). A hidden bespoke gutter profile is built into the edge profiles of the roof too.

Internally, variable profile widths of pine cladding accentuate the dramatic 5° slope. "It was all about making sure the roof has a thin profile," says Alastair – so much so that it tapers away on the external (overhanging) elements (as the insulation wasn't required).

The bedrooms enjoy both excellent exterior views and luxurious en suite bathrooms

FACT FILE

Name: Mike and Ann Urwin
Area: Argyll
Build type: Self-build
Size: 607m²
Build date: Jan–Sept 2013

Land cost: £0 (already owned)
Build cost: £500,000
Cost/m²: £1,483
House value: £750,000

CONTACTS

Architect Alastair MacIntyre
at McInnes Gardner Architects
(mcinnesgardner.co.uk
0141 332 3841)
Engineer Clancy Consulting Ltd
(0141 222 1720)
Contractor James Smith &
Company (07785 537060)
Joinery Willie Lewis
(01866 822359)
Steelwork Mackay Steelwork
and Cladding (01862 843910)
**Sky-Frame windows and
CR Laurence external glass
balcony** Gray & Dick
(0141 952 9619)
NorDan windows Kerri Philp
Showroom/Retail Coordinator
(01592 776922)
Stove Charnwood

(01983 537777)
Main doors Silvelox (silvelox.co.uk)
Internal doors Emerald Doors
(01422 387331)
Stone cladding Fernhill Stone
(0870 224 7201)
**Ground-source heat pump and
underfloor heating** Renewables
Now (01631 720587)
Waste treatment Balmoral
Tanks Direct (01224 859250)
Timber cladding Russwood
(01540 673648)
Render K-Rend
(028 2826 3303)
Single-ply roofing SRS Roofing
(0141 551 9555)
**Mechanical ventilation heat-
recovery (MVHR system)**
Villavent UK (01993 778481)

FLOORPLAN

LOWER GROUND FLOOR

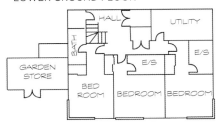

GROUND FLOOR

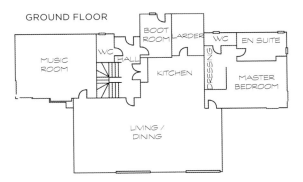

This new home has been built into its hillside setting and in order to make the most of its loch views, the open plan living accommodation has been placed on the top floor, including the master bedroom which benefits from an en suite with separate WC and dressing area. Thanks to the use of wrap-around glazing, all of the loch-facing rooms on the ground floor open out on to external terraces. The lower ground floor houses the guest accommodation and utility room.

The architect's view

While the building is modern, the materials and colours used in its elevations are intended to offer a degree of camouflage. It is 'of the land', minimising its visual impact in the landscape by avoiding the usual 'white render and grey slate' palette in favour of more muted natural colours in the stonework, 'khaki' render and timber panels.

The house sits in a shallow valley at the top of the site which became the source for the new roofscape – its angles reflecting the slopes on either side. The large glass box first floor hangs beneath the soaring roofs, landing on a suspended tray which becomes the external deck; the main bedroom floor sits below, wrapped in the hillside.

Silver Lining

Paul and Lesley Dadson have transformed a challenging
plot into the site of a new home that proves contemporary
design can be interesting and affordable

WORDS: ALEXANDRA PRATT PHOTOGRAPHY: NIGEL RIGDEN

This single-storey self-build is low in profile, but has been designed so as to capture the coastal view from the main living space. Its L-shaped design also provides privacy from neighbouring homes, and access to the semi-private courtyard from the living space. The exterior is clad in Marley Eternit's Equitone natura fibre-cement boards, while the granite paving, sourced from Nu-Stone, continues the clean lines of the architecture

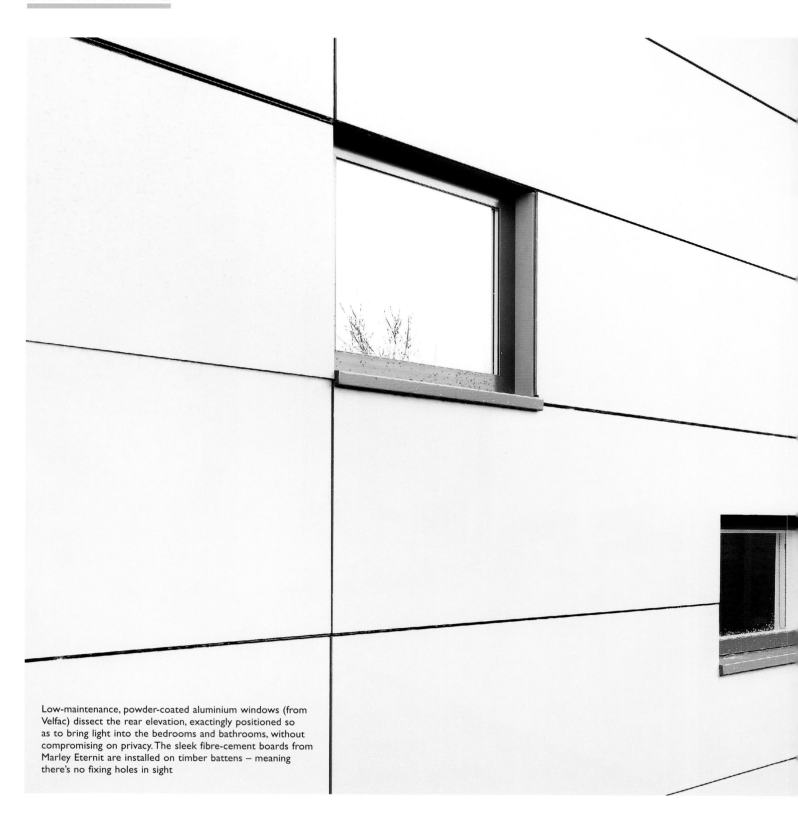

Low-maintenance, powder-coated aluminium windows (from Velfac) dissect the rear elevation, exactingly positioned so as to bring light into the bedrooms and bathrooms, without compromising on privacy. The sleek fibre-cement boards from Marley Eternit are installed on timber battens – meaning there's no fixing holes in sight

SILVER LINING

The corner where the two sides of the L-shaped design meet provided a good place to position the entrance hall – off which the living space and bedrooms (including the master bedroom and main bathroom) lead. The couple decided on including a third bedroom, which replaced a planned utility, meaning the boiler and mechanical recovery heat ventilation system are now housed within cupboards in the entrance hall

After holidaying in St Ives for many years, Lesley and Paul Dadson started to think about buying a property in this picturesque town in west Cornwall, known for its artists who come for the unique light. Having self-built their main home in Taunton, however, a new project was the last thing on their minds. "But then we found this site," says Paul. "It was the view; we felt we could do something here."

The plot in question was a fairly tight piece of land at the end of a private no-through road, but crucially, it sits atop a hill overlooking the old town and the sweep of bay beyond. It threw up several issues, however, that needed to be resolved before Paul and Lesley could close the deal, and this process took almost a year. As is so often the case with private roads, there was uncertainty as to who was responsible for maintaining it, as well as problems regarding drainage, which crosses a neighbour's property. Getting services up to the site also proved a headache.

With the plot secured, Paul and Lesley turned their attention to the existing planning permission and decided to resubmit plans for their own design. Despite Paul's career as a conservation officer, the couple were firm in their desire for a contemporary build. "We knew what we wanted: something very light and minimal," says Lesley. The constraints of the site and location also meant the build had to remain compact, with a low ridge height. But there were advantages. "With no road frontage, we didn't have to worry about copying neighbours' styles," says Paul.

When looking around for a suitable architect, Paul and Lesley quickly found Neil Wall from local practice Studio West Architects. "He understands contemporary design and is on our wavelength," says Paul. Over the next three months, plans emerged for a crisp, modern single storey home with a flat roof, designed around the principle of making the view available from the living areas.

The unusual grey fibre-cement board cladding was an early choice in the design process, and Paul's inspiration was a contemporary slate-hung extension to the Victorian art gallery in nearby Newlyn. "The building is gorgeous," he says. That sharp, clean look is one he wanted to emulate. Although used frequently on agricultural and commercial buildings, their architect Neil had also previously used the product on a Grade II* listed building in the Devon town of Sidmouth.

"When Paul came across Marley Eternit's Equitone fibre-cement boards, the aesthetic detail of the house changed," adds Neil. "The horizontal panels informed the flat roof. This was useful both in terms of cost, but also in lowering the ridge height of the building and reducing massing." The slate-gray colour is reminiscent of traditional local roofs and walls, and

Introducing Natural Light

In addition to the wall of floor-to-ceiling glazing, there are rooflights and an impressive glazed corner window towards the rear wall, bringing natural light deep into the floorplan. Pocket lights, created by hiding LEDs in wall insets, create swashes of light

The architect's view

We designed the house to be single storey due to the planning considerations – but being all on one level also meant that it was possible to establish good relations between the rooms and outdoor space. This inside-outside connection, which has been at the heart of modern architecture for many decades, was one of Paul and Lesley's priorities from the outset.

Space was maximised on this urban plot by setting the house back in the north-west corner, leaving the site open to the preferred east and south sides for solar gain and for the stunning sea vista east over St Ives harbour.

A semi-private courtyard wrapped within two arms of the L-shaped building was pivotal to the success of this house. The one sea view was key to the placement of the courtyard and the open plan living, dining, kitchen space behind (west). Full-height glazing here makes the most of the view.

The other wing houses the three bedrooms – including the master with en suite – and a large family bathroom. The Dadsons wanted the master bedroom to have a relationship with the semi-private courtyard, so full-height glazing features here, too. There are very interesting visual connections from the living area to the master bedroom. The courtyard is orientated south and east for sun, with the rear of the two wings blocking the predominant westerly winds. The family bathroom and en suite sit on the rear west and north-facing elevation. One double bedroom faces the rear but also has full-height glazed sections with a view into a private landscaped garden area.

It was key that the internal floor area was minimal in order to minimise potential costs. It is a very efficient plan, at only 98m², providing three bedroom accommodation on one level.

formed an integral part of the case they presented to the local planning office, which was ultimately successful. It's all about 'material context', as Paul suggests.

The fibre-cement board is low maintenance, although it was quite a challenge to get the final look right. Setting out around the windows was fairly complex and Neil had to do individual calculations for each panel. In order to eliminate fixing holes in the panels, they attached battens to the structure to which they, in turn, attached the panels using structural adhesives.

The build also needed to be affordable. "The cost per square metre was fundamental," says Paul, who set the initial budget at £143,000 for a 98m² build. Neil produced several highly detailed drawings to get 'cost certainty' for the project. Although this budget puts the build in the 'affordable' bracket, their design ambitions also meant large areas of glazing and the fibre-cement cladding had to be included in that price. (The latter cost a weighty £18,000.)

Both finishes and the contemporary style formed part of the

objections made by the Town Council and neighbours. Despite this, after four months and some informal pre-application discussions, the Dadsons' plans were passed and the contract for a main contractor put out to tender, eventually going to local firm Level Construction. "It was too far away for us to project manage ourselves," explains Lesley.

A highly insulated timber frame was the construction system of choice. "It's quick and provides an airtight build," says architect Neil Wall. "I wouldn't think of anything else, due to the standards of insulation compared to wet methods," adds Paul. Together with Neil, the couple chose to use steels for the large spans across the sliding windows, sourced from Velfac, to the front.

The open plan nature of the main living room, which contains the kitchen and dining area, makes the most of the 98m² space in this house, and its views down to the coast. A light, neutral interior scheme (the white kitchen is from Magnet) helps in creating an illusion of space, while soft furnishings and wood flooring, from Woodstock, lends warmth

The windows allow for some passive solar gain, although the property is cosy largely thanks to a gas-fired boiler supplying the underfloor heating. A mechanical ventilation heat recovery system also keeps the air fresh with low humidity (as well as passing warm air to the bedrooms).

When it came to the interiors, the design morphed from two bedrooms into three, following the couple's decision to sacrifice the utility room. But this was compensated for by a clever use of storage space throughout. "I worked out where everything was going before the build," adds Lesley, who also designed the kitchen. She then sourced this from Magnet, plus some quality detailing and a granite worktop. This was paired with an inexpensive but chic bespoke aluminium splashback.

The pared-back style is continued throughout the interior, with clever detailing such as shadow gaps around the doors – in place of traditional architraves – and tall, elegant internal doors. This attention to detail and careful use of space certainly gives the property a high-spec feel, which belies the eventual budget of just £160,000 (the overrun due in large part to delays in the ground works during a wet winter).

The Dadsons plan to retire to the resulting contemporary house, but for the moment enjoy it as holiday home, and also let it out for others to enjoy. "We love it here... the light and the views," says Paul. "But I also loved the journey."

"When you do a house in white, you do need to inject colour and, for us, it comes from furnishings and artwork"

FLOORPLAN

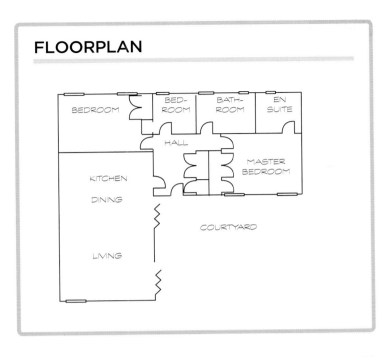

BEDROOM

BED-ROOM

BATH-ROOM

EN SUITE

HALL

MASTER BEDROOM

KITCHEN

DINING

COURTYARD

LIVING

FACT FILE

Name: Paul and Lesley Dadson
Area: Cornwall
Build type: Contemporary-style self-build
Size: 98m²
Build Date: Nov 2012–Oct 13

Land cost: £165,000
Build Cost: £160,000
Cost/m²: £1,633
House value: £425,000

CONTACTS

Architect Neil Wall of Studio West Architects (studiowestarchitects.co.uk; 01736 788892)
Kitchen Magnet (magnet.co.uk)
Main contractor Level Construction (01736 756204; levelconstruction.info)
Up-and-over window Timber Tek (timber-tek.co.uk)
Cladding Marley Eternit Equitone Natura fibre-cement panels (marleyeternit.co.uk; 01283 722588)
Wood flooring Woodstock

(wood-stock.co.uk)
Electrician Tristan Weidner (07966 663837)
Bathrooms Victoria Plumb (victoriaplumb.com)
Doors and windows Velfac (velfac.co.uk)
Underfloor heating Timoleon Toron System (timoleon.co.uk)
External granite paving Nu-Stone (nustone.co.uk)
Gate-maker Richard Johns (01736 333412)

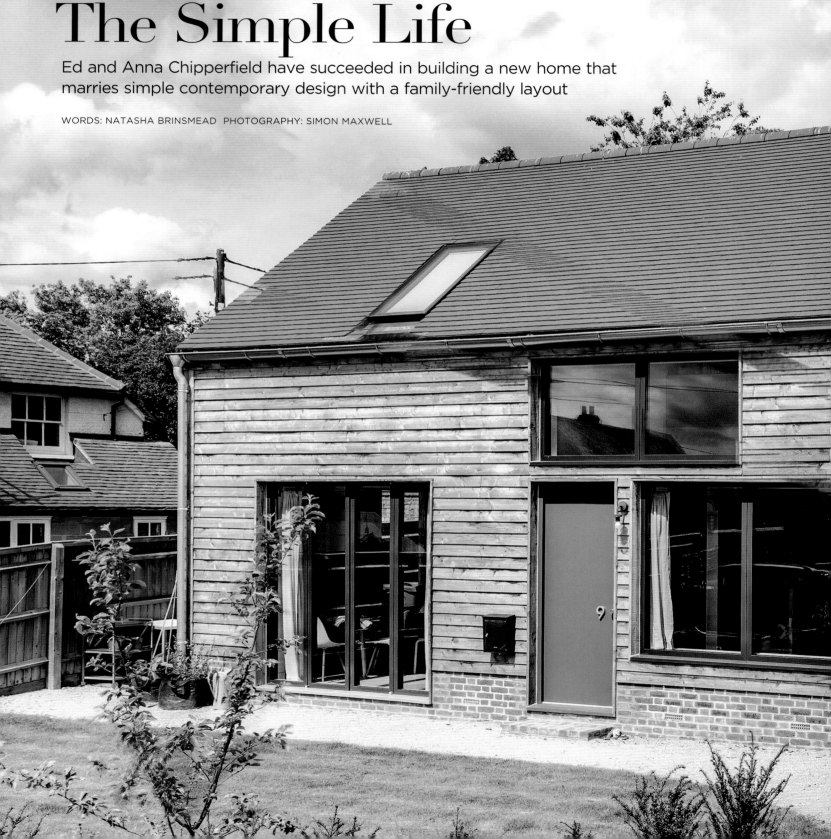

The Simple Life

Ed and Anna Chipperfield have succeeded in building a new home that marries simple contemporary design with a family-friendly layout

WORDS: NATASHA BRINSMEAD   PHOTOGRAPHY: SIMON MAXWELL

The long, open layout of the house was something Ed and Anna were really keen on. The partially polished concrete floor retains so much heat that visitors assume they have underfloor heating. This raw, industrial feel is continued through the birch-faced ply walls, staircase and finishing touches, whilst the huge Velfac windows and double-height hallway bring in plenty of natural light

Ground Floor Spaces
The open-plan ground floor allows for light to flood through the various living areas while also allowing the couple to keep an eye on their young son Jasper. In the living area, a Morsø stove offers a heat source, while Ed's office is divided off from this space. He got this idea from industrial factories where the foreman has an office sectioned off from the main areas

Viking longhouse meets New York loft apartment." This is how Ed Chipperfield describes the new home he and wife Anna have built in rural Buckinghamshire. It's not often you hear a new home described in such a way, but then again this is a house that is surprising on many levels.

After renovating and living in a Victorian house in Oxford, Ed and Anna came to the conclusion that period houses weren't their thing. They put their house on the market and sold it almost immediately. The Chipperfields found a building plot which had been split into three; Ed and Anna's parcel of land originally being an orchard on the site. Despite being up against a number of developers, the fact that they had already sold their own house – as well as the owners of the plot planning to still live on part of the original plot themselves – worked in the couple's favour.

While the plot came with outline permission for a more traditional timber frame house, Ed and Anna knew that they were after a more contemporary design. And although a covenant restricting the house's height had been placed on the plot – which sits within a Conservation Area – the new design was passed by the planners.

"I like history and I have a bit of a thing about Viking longhouses," explains Ed of the concept behind the new house design. "We have friends with a house on the Isle of Skye and really like the style – they offer an open plan, long but useful space, with the bedrooms located in the eaves (a happy coincidence given that there were planning restrictions on the ridge height of the new building). So that was our influence.

"Anna and I both grew up in the Eighties and were influenced by all those warehouse conversions that were everywhere at the time," continues Ed. "We basically kept pecking away at the original design

Kitchen Diner
The IKEA kitchen, like the rest of the house, is minimally fitted out, with a crisp white island unit housing the hob, oven and storage

until we had something we were both happy with – a raw, cabin-like freestanding structure."

The couple chose architect Kieran Hawkins, a friend of the family, from Mailen Design to come up with the design for their new home. "We wanted a young architect with similar ideas to us," explains Ed. "We found that a lot of the local architects we approached only wanted to do conventional things, but Kieran brought a fresh approach to the design."

Kieran takes up the story: "We tried hard to avoid transplanting a slick city house into historic Buckinghamshire. Our aim was to construct a home that had the clarity and strength of an agricultural building while providing an uplifting backdrop to daily life for this particular family."

The result is a house that is both modern and understated, yet incorporates rustic and traditional materials that allow it to blend into its surroundings. It has been clad in Scottish larch which fitted Ed and Anna's ideal of a low-maintenance home; it requires no treatment and has been left to weather to a silver grey.

Structural insulated panels (SIPs) were chosen as the method of construction for the new house, with Ed and Anna keen on the idea of the fast build times they offered as well as the superior thermal performance. "SIPs construction provides excellent environmental performance and allowed the structure to be erected to watertight stage in only one week. The panels were great, but the installers were messy – we had to hire a skip after they left," explains Ed.

"I'd definitely recommend SIPs. The construction was really fast and there were no joists and beams to contend with either, meaning it is a

good option for open plan spaces," adds Ed.

The couple employed Les McKeran from Link Development & Groundworks as the main contractor, who worked alongside Ed and Kieran throughout the build. "Les really is one in a million," says Ed. "From day one, if Les said it would happen, it did."

During the relatively short build – the whole project, from conception to moving in took around 10 months – Ed and Anna avoided renting, staying at their friend's cottage on the Isle of Skye for two months and with family for the remaining eight months. "If we did it again, we might rent," reflects Ed. "It would have been nice to have been a bit closer to the project at times when decisions were needed fast."

It was during their time staying with family and friends that Ed and Anna began paring everything down. "Most of our belongings went into storage during the build. When we were ready to move in, we realised that we really hadn't missed a single thing – so we gave away loads of stuff."

Throughout the build, specifications were all based on Ed and Anna's ethos that: "Each decision you make should move you towards a simpler life." This 'simplification' of their everyday lives is very much reflected in the entire design of the house. Agricultural and industrial finishes have been used throughout, from the partially polished concrete floors and unfinished birch-faced ply details, to the choice of glazing and heating system.

"We considered underfloor heating but decided that it wasn't worth it," explains Ed. "The concrete floor has been poured extra thick (around four feet) and provides a huge thermal mass. The windows bathe the concrete floor all day with heat and in the evening they are so warm underfoot that everyone assumes we have underfloor heating anyway." The house is actually heated via a tiny condensing gas boiler and radiators, and due to the construction, with an additional layer of insulation in the walls, the couple find themselves with heating bills of around just £300 per year.

With the three bedrooms located in the eaves to maximise space on the ground floor, the upper level offers a cosy space to retreat to without feeling cramped. A bridge over the entrance hall connects the master suite with the other bedrooms and family bathroom, and similar raw materials have been used in this area of the home too. The sanitaryware in the master en suite is from Duravit

"We are always open to sustainable ways of doing things," says Ed, "but we also wanted to get the best value. We looked at solar panels and it didn't add up. We thought about heat exchangers but they weren't for us. We craved simplicity and felt that building a house should be as simple as possible – I can't think of anything worse than having a plant room!" Double as opposed to triple glazing from Velfac has been used throughout as the couple simply didn't feel the need to overspecify.

Internally, the layout is dominated by one long open plan space which is double-height in places. To break up the open plan arrangement the floor levels have been varied between the kitchen diner and the living area – the living area sits 30cm below ground level, with the step up to the kitchen providing a handy extra place to sit when required.

In fact, this house features many clever design ideas for such an unfussy project. On the ground floor, partitions featuring glass and ply form a separate yet connected home office for Ed, a commercial copywriter, to work from home. Meanwhile on the first floor, two of the three bedrooms feature internal windows that open out over the double-height stairwell providing a nice link between the master bedroom and Jasper's room. "They are cheeky little things," says Ed.

The architect's view

Anna and Ed were great clients. They gave us guidelines of what they wanted and what they didn't want, but were very open to our ideas as their architects. The final design was the result of a thorough conversation between architect and client to achieve a building that neither of us would have been able to design without the other.

The final design is a contemporary building that was built within the constraints of a conservative outline planning permission. Planning is a political process and is always unpredictable. To satisfy both the local council, who wanted a traditional barn-style cottage, and the clients, who wanted a free-flowing work of modern architecture, was a real achievement and led to a building that is not compromised, but is richer for accommodating these competing demands.

The interiors have a high degree of variety while minimising the number of interior walls to ensure that areas flow into each other, with changes in floor level, double-height spaces and views from one room to another all carefully managed. The split-level design was important to provide a generosity of space and a sense of connection.

When you enter the house, you are presented with views across the whole ground floor, and upwards to the bedrooms and through the rooflights to the trees and clouds beyond.

The hatches felt right from the first time we sketched them. They allow the clients to enjoy the double-height hallway from their bedrooms and to connect the first floor and ground floor in a way that gives them options of varying privacy levels. They also enable parents and child to talk, play games or read stories without leaving their own rooms.

"We can open them up and let music from our room stream through the whole house – they are also a good way of letting natural light flow through the spaces."

For much of the raw, clean style that has been achieved throughout the internal spaces, Ed praises their carpenter who crafted all the exposed ply features of the house – including the ingenious birch ply cover for the extractor hood in the kitchen, and the built-in elements that make up the bathroom. "He came up with loads of ideas and we trusted him as he has really good taste."

Furnished simply with predominantly original mid-century modern furniture ("the house was basically designed to suit our love of this style of furniture," laughs Ed) the house manages to exude comfort and charm through its individual touches and tailored design features. The finished project is certainly a lesson in pared-down living done well.

FLOORPLAN

GROUND FLOOR

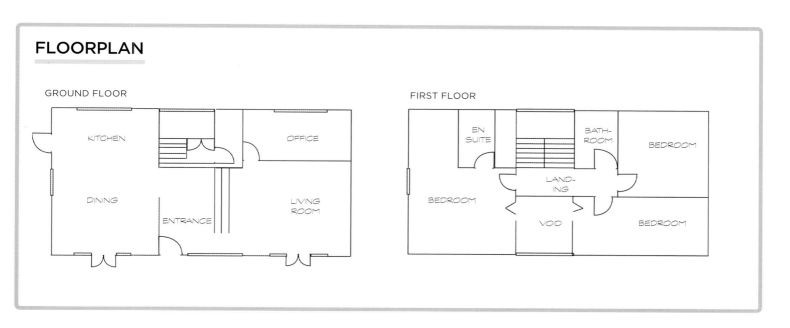

FIRST FLOOR

FACT FILE

Name: Ed and Anna Chipperfield
Area: Buckinghamshire
Build type: Self-build
Size: 170m²
Build date: April 2013–May 14

House cost: £302,000
Build cost: £270,000
Cost/m²: £1,588
House value: £675,000

CONTACTS

Architect Kieran Hawkins of Mailen Design (mailendesign.com, 020 3735 5880)
Main contractor, builder, carpenter and concrete flooring Link Development & Groundworks Ltd (01869 323140)
Birch-faced ply Travis Perkins (travisperkins.co.uk)
SIPs and insulation Kingspan (kingspan.co.uk)
Glazing and patio doors Velfac (01223 897100)

Rooflights The Rooflight Company (01993 833155
Kitchen IKEA (ikea.com)
Worktops James Latham (lathamtimber.co.uk)
Bathrooms Duravit (duravit.co.uk)
Woodburning stove Morsø. (morso.co.uk)
Roof tiles Markey Eternit (marleyeternit.co.uk)
Larch cladding Russwood (01540 673648)

"We kept pecking away at the design until we had something we were both happy with: a raw, cabin-like freestanding structure"

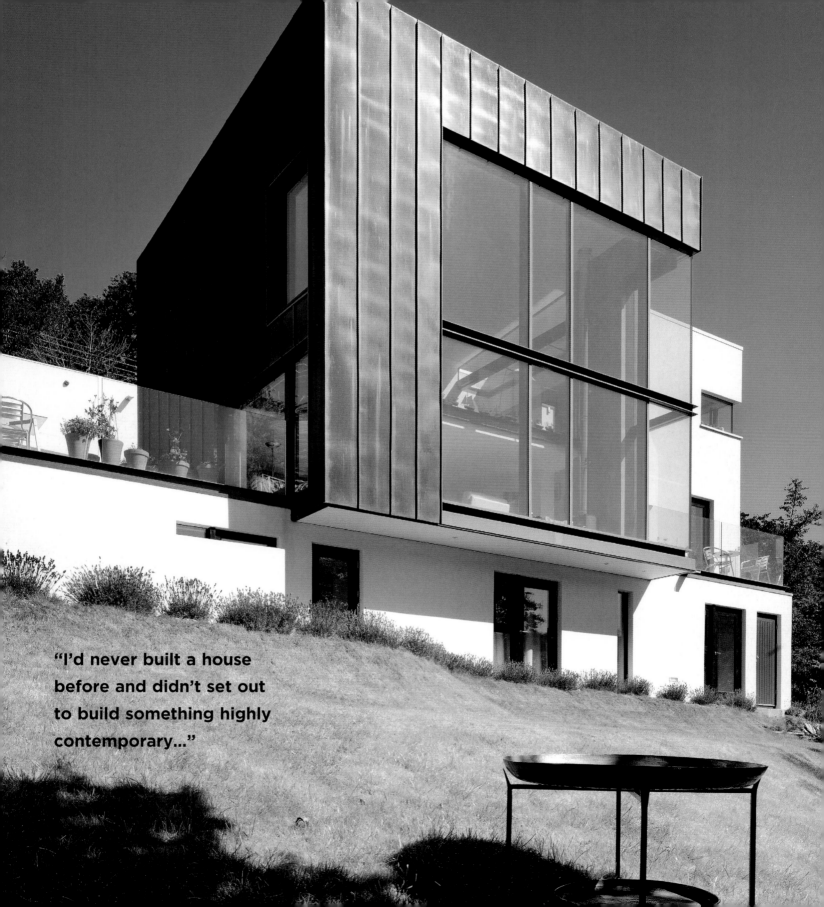

"I'd never built a house
before and didn't set out
to build something highly
contemporary..."

The Hangout

Andrew Beveridge's award-winning waterside
home is a masterclass in modern living

WORDS: JUDE WEBLEY   PHOTOGRAPHY: NIGEL RIGDEN

"I held a beauty contest for four local architects, which Stan Bolt won because of his stunning ideas and the sheer effort he put in ... the site was the primary influence on the form, materials and detailing of the design"

Looking Out

A double-height living room, made possible by the steel-frame construction, takes maximum advantage of the spectacular location and views. Situating the living accommodation in the upper storeys not only makes the most of the stunning views; it also responds practically to the sloping nature of the site. The building is accessed from the high side of the plot, away from the river, so the entrance is at the top of the house

Dining Area

A mezzanine level looks down through a double-height void to the living room below. Copper light fittings echo the external cladding, while the walls have been lined with panels of laminated oak to bring warmth to the interior and contrast with the white render

The Devon village of Newton Ferrers is glowingly described by the region's tourist board as 'a little slice of tranquillity just 10 miles from the urban sprawl of Plymouth,' and 'a hidden gem with a secret, tranquil atmosphere'. These aren't idle boasts. Surrounded by ancient woodland, the village sits on the banks of the Newton Creek and offers everything you'd expect from a picture-postcard idyll, including thatched cottages and a pub at its centre.

No wonder Andrew Beveridge chose this spot as the perfect place in which to enjoy his retirement and life beside the water. But his migration south from Aberdeen to the West Country brought with it something with which Newton Ferrers had previously been totally unfamiliar: contemporary architecture. For when Andrew purchased a traditional timber framed bungalow on a vertiginous site directly overlooking the creek, his decision to build a highly modern replacement dwelling initially caused uproar in the local community.

"There were 64 letters of objection and not one person backed the scheme," he recalls. "The site already had planning approval for a traditional two storey house, but it wasn't something I wanted to build."

Once Andrew's initial planning application had been refused in July 2008, an appeal submission was lodged and planning permission was finally approved in November of the same year. A construction package was then put out to tender and work began on site in April 2009 to build the controversial three storey home, which was designed specifically for its setting by award-winning architect Stan Bolt – whose practice has developed a reputation for imaginative, site-specific work in the south west of England.

"I held a beauty contest for four local architects, which Stan won because of his stunning ideas and the sheer effort he put in," explains Andrew. "I'd never built a house before and didn't set out to build something highly contemporary, but when I saw some of Stan's other houses, I knew he would design something exciting for the site."

Stan Bolt appreciates Thirties Modernism and his designs reflect this fact. He is also familiar with tricky planning situations, and Andrew Beveridge's extremely loose brief ("I wanted a four bedroom house on three floors – that was about it") gave him the perfect opportunity to flex his creative muscles and create a truly show-stopping waterside home.

Clad externally in a combination of render and copper, The Green House takes full advantage of its dramatic position overlooking the estuary. "I've always wanted to have a house beside the sea, but although I looked around at plots and properties in Scotland, I decided that the water wasn't quite warm enough up there," laughs Andrew, who enjoys sailing and previously ran a company which operated remotely controlled submarines in the

Looking Out
A double-height living room, made possible by the steel-frame construction, takes maximum advantage of the spectacular location and views

The Kitchen
The working area of the kitchen is divided from the dining space by a stairwell, and has been fitted with simple white cabinets from B&Q with black Corian worktops

North Sea. Now semi-retired, he lives with his partner Sally, and was keen that the new house would be accessible and inviting for their children and grandchildren.

Living in Aberdeen meant that site visits were relatively limited – and Andrew was crossing the Atlantic in his boat during nine months of the 18-month build project – but he enjoyed monitoring progress and liaised with the project architect, Nick Elkins, throughout the work. He was also active in choosing fixtures and fittings for the new house, and was keen that the building be as sustainable as possible.

Space and water heating demands are met through a combination of passive low-tech provisions, such as insulation and orientation, teamed with new technologies. A combined heat and power (CHP) boiler – which was only the third to be used in this country at the time of installation – is employed in combination with solar panels for water heating. Heating for the internal space is delivered through an underfloor heating coil, and photovoltaic panels generate electricity.

"Strangely, the bungalow was already called The Green House when I bought it, but the name suits its replacement perfectly," smiles Andrew.

When the main contractor went into liquidation one third of the way through the project, the build grounded to a sudden halt. "When

Site-specific design

The Green House stands on the northern bank of Newton Creek in an Area of Outstanding Natural Beauty, and serves as a full stop to the ribbon of predominantly 20th-century village developments.

The site was the primary influence on the form, materials and detailing of the design by architect Stan Bolt, and the vertical arrangement over three storeys was a direct response to the steep gradient of the land.

Inverting the plan allows entry into the house from the highest level via a bridge and Stan's trademark oversized, pivoting, oak entrance door.

Living areas are arranged in a horizontal and vertical open plan arrangement. The double-storey space takes advantage of the estuary views and maximises the penetration of sunlight to the rear of the building.

Living spaces are contained in a highly insulated, steel-framed structure, clad externally in copper, which cantilevers over a rendered blockwork lower ground floor. Bedroom accommodation on the lower level is contained in a robust rendered, masonry plinth set into the contours of the site, and its roof forms a terrace for the living accommodation above. "I would have made the master bedroom on the middle floor slightly wider," Andrew concedes, looking back. "But that's the only thing I would change."

Varying floor heights and connecting stairs replicate the form of the natural landscape outside, which slopes down to the water. An abstract array of rooflights, windows and door openings suit this freeform arrangement.

Retaining the foreshore vegetation and green landscape has further enabled this bold new house to sit comfortably in its sensitive setting.

the first building contractor went into liquidation, it caused delays and increased the overall budget, which nobody could have foreseen. It was definitely the low point of the whole project."

However, work resumed three months later, when a new contractor was appointed. Andrew then moved into the unfinished house on Christmas Eve 2010 and lived there while building work continued around him until early February 2011.

"When I first moved in, I was worried about the locals' reaction to the house, but people have seen how it blends into the landscape and many have been won over," says Andrew. "I bought this site for the river views, but there's also a wonderful view east which couldn't previously be appreciated from the old bungalow. Building up above the tree line opened up a magnificent outlook over the typical Devon countryside. Now, I can enjoy my retirement looking out at these amazing views in a home where I plan to remain for the rest of my life."

FLOORPLAN

An entrance bridge leads into the open plan kitchen and mezzanine dining area, which is divided by a staircase to the ground floor living room below. The master bedroom and en suite bathroom are also located on the ground floor level, with three further bedrooms on the lower ground floor. All principal rooms have been orientated to face towards the water.

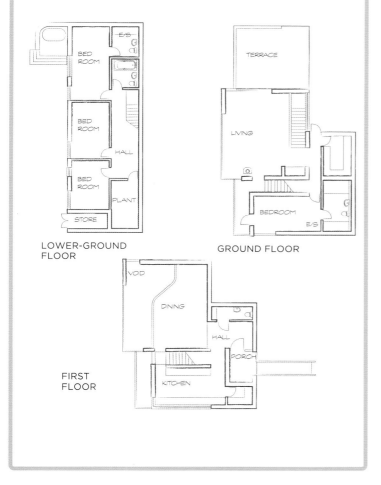

LOWER-GROUND FLOOR

GROUND FLOOR

FIRST FLOOR

FACT FILE

Name: Andrew Beveridge
Area: Devon
Build type: Self-build
Size: 250m²
Build date: Aug 2009–Feb 11

Plot cost: £550,000
Build cost: £800,000
Cost/m²: £3,200
Total cost: £13,050
House value: £1,350,000

CONTACTS

Architect Stan Bolt (01803 852588; stanboltarchitect.com)
Structural engineer John Grimes Partnership (01752 690533)
Services consultant Vortech (0845 867 4756)
Second contractor Bovey Construction (01626 821919)
Flat roof David Williams (01647 277258)
Copper cladding A & S Roofing (01837 810287)
Mechanical work WH Joce & Son (01752 668381)
Electrics Wannels Electrotechnical System (01392 874281)
Steel fabricators Eden Engineering (01752 840783)
External glazing and balustrades Solaglas Architectural systems (0117 902 1000)
Waterproofing to structural slabs and retaining walls Grace Construction Products (01925 855330)
RoofKrete Flat Roof Waterproofing System Krete Sustain Systems (07970 455050)

D-line ironmongery Allgood plc (020 7387 9951)
Engineered oak floors Kährs (kahrs.com)
Slate flooring Delabole Slate Company (01840 212242)
Slate slabs Kenmart Timber & Slate Products (01626 833564)
Blinds Silent Gliss (01843 863571)
Ecogen micro-CHP boiler Baxi (baxi.co.uk)
Sanitaryware Roca (uk.roca.com)
Taps VOLA UK (01525 720111)
Showers Grohe (0871 200 3414)
Bathroom tiles Royal Mosa (07825 957000; 0207 490 0484)
Towel radiators Zehnder Group UK (01276 605855)
Light fittings Amos Lighting (01392 677030)
Precast concrete Mexboro (01803 558025)
Stove Firebelly Stoves (01422 375582)
Solar thermal panels Fischer Fixings UK (01491 827900)
Kitchen B&Q (diy.com)

"Despite some local residents' initial opposition to the scheme, the house blends with its landscape and has grown in popularity since its completion"

House of Fun

Matt and Sophie White have created an impressive
low-energy, high-design family home on a tight
site in London – with a refreshingly light tough

WORDS: JASON ORME PHOTOGRAPHY: SIMON MAXWELL

Ultra-thin insulation

Matt used nanogel – now rebranded as aerogel – insulation for his home. It's effectively a gel in which the liquid component has been replaced with a gas – making it ultra-light. Long regarded as one of the most effective insulating materials in the world, aerogel consists largely (95 per cent) of air contained in a structure, with pore sizes less than the free path of air molecules - meaning that heat transfer is severely inhibited. As such, it is also 100 per cent moisture resistant and a highly effective acoustic insulator. It achieves a U value of 0.64/m²K per 25mm².

In terms of application, it usually comes laminated to a solid board – in Matt's case GRP, but other common options include magnesium silicate board. Typically, a combined board of just 59mm will achieve a U value of 0.29 (it would take an expanded polystyrene equivalent double the thickness to achieve a similar U value). It can be used for floors, walls or loft/roof applications too.

Matt White is destined to become one of the architecture world's great new stars, and if his newly completed home, which he shares with wife Sophie and children Daisy, Mia and Arthur, in Shepherd's Bush is anything to go by, it will be a happier world, too. For Matt has created a home that displays many things: considerable nouse when it comes to spotting a rare and potentially lucrative opportunity; a talent for maximising a small urban site for purposes of light, comfortable family living; and, most pleasingly, a feeling that – given the ability to think about every last corner of the house and every last little bit of lifestyle choice – homes can be playful, fun and hugely enjoyable. Architecture is at worst a serious, pretentious, stuffy business - this home, unlike others, raises a smile and hits its many targets every time.

"We bought the Victorian end-of-terrace house next door (Number 25) in 2005," begins Matt. The garden plot that would later become Number 23 had a separate title, and while we fancied our chances of being able to take adverse possession of the property, there was always the risk of someone coming along and taking ownership. Incredibly, given the lack of land in London, the problematic legal standing of the land seemed to depress the value of Number 25. So in many ways, we were paid a premium to take on the house with a potential building plot next door."

With 7m of frontage and 12m deep, the site is around 20 per cent smaller than that of its neighbouring properties, but Matt and Sophie could see the huge potential it offered for a sustainable family home with contemporary living space. "We knew that we wanted to get as much space out of the site as possible, but we also wanted something that would, in its simplest form, have low running costs and would also be a fun, surprising and practical

Matt has managed to include a small outdoor area, accessed from the living space. The Wendy house folds away completely into the wall). Some 40m² of triple glazing fills the house with natural light

Kitchen

The vertical windows allow the family to look out and retain privacy at the same time (as can be seen in the photos of the front elevation). Recessed, low-energy LED lighting allows subtle washes of light. Hidden storage is a key feature of the house – not least a remarkable stowaway drinks cabinet (above) sourced from a club Matt was working on

First Floor

Automated rooflights from Sunsquare are finished with automated blackout blinds (from Waverley) for flexible light and ventilation in the first floor rooms. The engineered oak boards, with a natural oiled finish, are from Wood 'n' Beyond

Adverse possession

Adverse possession is a complex part of property law and is designed around the proviso that property should serve a useful purpose. Commonly known as 'squatter's rights', in simple terms it enables a 'squatter' to apply for title ownership of land after a period of 10 years if the land has already been registered (12 years if the land is unregistered).

Matt and Sophie bought the end-of-terrace house in West London with the aim of later taking adverse possession of the 77m² bit of land next door. This complex legal situation appeared to put many people off, but Matt and Sophie saw the opportunity to benefit from the land if they could sort out the title. When they came to investigate the property as a whole, they realised that the land had been registered under possessory title for, "something like 23 years," according to Matt. "Much legal wrangling later, we then acquired the benefit of that title."

family home," explains Matt.

Able to live next door while construction progressed, the Whites packaged out the project to a main contractor who could easily be supervised. A basement was essential to the 'maxing-out' part of the remit but, cleverly, Matt allowed space for a sunken lightwell garden to the rear elevation, filling this whole lower level – used as a playroom and office space – with light. The rest of the house is built out of open panel timber frame surrounded in ultra-thin aerogel panels, clad in glass-reinforced plastic (GRP) which is covered in a render mix of sand and a bonding agent, and then painted. "We were aware that, being in an urban environment and close to the street, we needed a covering that could be restored if it was interfered with, for example by graffiti. Not that it has happened, but it could just be painted over."

The fact that the front of the house and street abut each other so starkly could have potentially created a problem - solved by one of Matt's many clever design touches. As anyone with young children will know, one of the main annoyances of life in general is storage of the pushchair (or 'travel system'). It always ends up hanging round the door with its massive frame blocking hallways and cluttering the place up. Matt came up with a brilliant solution: effectively, 23 Keith Grove has two front doors - one has access to a small storage area, big enough to fit a pushchair, which can be accessed from inside but closed off too. So you never again have to look at the bloody great big buggy when the kids have gone to bed.

Simple improvements in design soon add up to making the whole environment happier, too. Hidden storage is a key theme, with each of the three children having their own desk/shelving space in the basement play area - "It means that when all the doors are opened up, they can't steal things off each other!" says Matt. There's also a brilliant stowaway drinks cabinet, automated blackout blinds in all bedrooms, a Jack and Jill en suite, LED lighting that looks great for parties and, the coup de grâce, a doorbell that doesn't just ring but also illuminates a charming 'Hello!' magically embedded within the render.

Externally, the house is undeniably contemporary in flavour but, as Matt claims, does aim to nod in the direction of the local housing stock. For a start, in form, it's undeniably similar to the late Georgian houses nearby; it's submissive to them in terms of scale (despite

offering more living space) and also replicative in terms of colour. A huge front window, jettying out over the street, features electro-opaque glass that ensures varying degrees of privacy at the touch of a button (indeed a lot of the house is very much touch-button friendly).

Privacy glass

Electro-opaque glass (where a current runs through the glass to turn it frosted) has been around for a few years, but Matt achieved the same frosted-at-the-touch-of-a-button effect with a film which adheres to the inside of a regular glazing panel. The system used here is called ProDisplay Intelligent Glass and it's supplied through a range of UK outlets (many 'window film' suppliers don't offer switchable versions). It's a self-adhesive DIY film common in commercial situations, that operates with a pre-programmed RF remote on-off switch (between frosted and clear) and comes in two standard widths (980mm and 1,200mm) – although most suppliers will create custom size films. The coated polyester films tend to come with guarantees lasting at least 10 years and can be cleaned with a damp cloth. Generally, the films are considered to diminish natural light levels by somewhere between 5-15 per cent and some of the films do claim to have energy-saving benefits too. The film can also be used to turn glass into a high-definition rear projection TV screen.

FLOORPLAN

BASEMENT

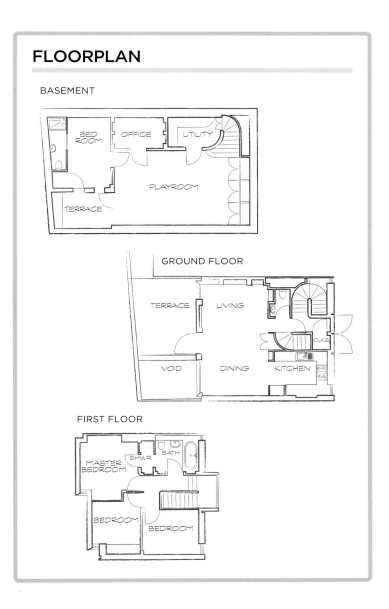

GROUND FLOOR

FIRST FLOOR

FACT FILE

Name: Matt White and Sophie Elmarie Ward
Area: West London
Build type: Self-buildl
Size: 159m²

Build date: Jan 2012–June 13
Land cost: £0 (adverse possession)
Build cost: £525,000
Cost/m²: £3,302
House value: £2m

CONTACTS

Design MATT Architecture (020 3490 1243 mattarchitecture.com
Main contractors MI Builders Limited (mibltd.co.uk)
Rainwater harvesting system Halsted Rain (020 8318 0957
Rooflights Sunsquare (0845 226 3172
Stainless steel mirror Elite Metalcraft (020 8810 5122
Switchable glass film ProDisplay Intelligent Glass (0870 766 8437)

Terrace tiles Solus Ceramics (0121 753 0777
Glass (black façade) AGC Glass Europe (01788 535353)
Ironmongery Trapex Hardware Ltd (01992 462150)
LED lighting and remotes World of LEDs (0116 268 2288)
Light pipes Solatube (01234 241466)
Moulded spotlight surrounds Tornado (020 8788 2324)

"We're delighted with what we've achieved," says Matt. "It's a great family house in a central location that suits our lifestyles brilliantly. It's light, cheap to run and feels very spacious given the constraints we have had to face."

It's also a triumph because it's an example of the positive force of good architecture. If you could devote this much time and thought to making your house really work for you, reflecting your laid-back and clever personality so well, then you'd be a convert too. So rarely do we see homes which have been so intensively designed. And when we do, they really stand out.

Sound & Vision

A Seventies bungalow is transformed thanks to
a clever scheme of small extensions, external
makeover and internal remodel

WORDS: JASON ORME PHOTOGRAPHY: BRETT CHARLES

The new house replaces a run-down stone cottage and
enjoys 270 deg panoramic views over open countryside.
The patio area, accessed from the glazed rear, has been
raised to allow views over the stone wall. The structure
is a mix of cavity blockwork to the stone-clad front
elevation, and steel frame to the main part of the house

Front Elevation
Western red cedar boards, left untreated, have been simply fixed to the curves on the front elevation. Due to the presence of bats, two bat cassettes, with slit entrances, were incorporated into the void between the cladding and the blockwork. Hidden mortar joints (mortar is used to keep the stone together, but only to a depth where it can't be seen) have been used to give the appearance of modern drystone walling

O rganic buildings are the strength and lightness of the spiders' spinning, buildings qualified by light, bred by native character to everyone and married to the ground." If ever Frank Lloyd Wright's guidance about successful organic architecture could be relevant to building one-off homes in Britain in the early 21st century, then it's here, for the fabulous Carreg a Gwydr (Welsh for Stone and Glass) – a masterly self-build in the countryside outside Chepstow that is the pride and joy of its owners, Tim and Ceridwen Coulson, and its architect, Martin Hall of Hall + Bednarczyk.

It all started off with a vision; as everything great must. The owners could see past the tired mid-Fifties house already on the site to the views – a dreamy 270 deg vista of private farmland. The large plot sat on the edge of a small settlement within an Area of Outstanding Natural Beauty (AONB). With strict policies on replacement in place (initially up to no more than 30 per cent extra volume was allowed), they turned to Hall + Bednarczyk (who had already won a RIBA Award in 2011 for the four-bed home 'Blue Door') for help. "We initially interviewed three local architects from the Chepstow area and felt that Martin and Kelly [Bednarczyk] would give us the best chance to achieve our goals," says Tim. "They were very much the new babes on the block but they clearly had a far better idea of what we were hoping to achieve on the site.

"We then spent an evening with Martin and Kelly, and over a couple of bottles of fine wine we went through a slideshow of contemporary architecture of houses from around the world and we picked out features that we liked. It might just have been a wall in one photo or a flight of stairs in another and we slowly gave them ideas of what we hoped to achieve. We stipulated that the house should be built of natural products such as stone, glass and wood – preferably recycling the stone from the original cottage, although this wasn't achieved. We then gave them free rein to come up with a design. They have a very distinctive 'look' to their designs so we had an idea of what to expect. We were very happy with the design from the word go and are quick to make decisions, so went with the original design with only a few interior alterations."

To manage any potential overheating on the south-facing back of the house (above), large overhanging roof eaves and balconies were designed. They shield the interior from the high midday sun in summer, while allowing the low winter sun to penetrate

A green house

The house has impeccable green credentials. Loops for a 12kW NIBE ground-source heat pump are buried in the large front garden, while a secondary heat exchanger pre-heats the water for the 300-litre hot water cylinder. There's also a mechanical ventilation unit with heat recovery (MVHR) but the house operates a passive ventilation system, too, incorporating a rooflight that automatically opens when the temperature reaches a certain level, to allow air to move through the house

The Staircase

In order to remove the need for stringers, which would have spoiled the elegant effect somewhat, a single piece of steel zig zags through the bespoke oak staircase, providing support

"Tim and Ceridwen wanted modern, but not too modern," explains Martin Hall. "We knew that we needed to maximise the potential of the site both in spatial terms and to take full advantage of the views. The new house would be in the same position as the old and the solution was to use natural materials where possible to the public-facing (front) elevation, with a private rear elevation dominated by glass."

Because of the tight restrictions on volume, they decided to maximise the habitable space through the use of very low-pitched (practically flat) roofs and the inclusion of a basement. The north-facing front elevation has been clad in a mix of 175mm-thick sandstone, sourced from a local quarry, cut and laid with hidden joints to create a contemporary drystone wall effect, and western redcedar, laid horizontally. Minimal openings to this elevation create a sense of privacy and contrast with the flared, open glass frontage of the south-

facing rear, which incorporates overhangs to take the worst of the heat of the midday sun off the windows. The sandstone wall is a 75mm double blockwork cavity wall (with the stone an extra skin); the rest of the house is built off a steel frame, for its strength and slender lines.

All of which rather begs the question – how contemporary is it? In a way this house is defined by what it isn't as well as what it is. It doesn't attempt to recreate an existing style, so it's not 'period' in that sense. Yet it doesn't really conform to our notion of what a modern house might look like either – namely white render and harsh, straight lines. But its principles are very much of the moment, being sensitive to its surroundings, with its low, horizontal form merging with the landscape, and its use of modern steel and glass to suck in all of that view. The curves, the softer feel and the natural materials make this a rural home, effectively, and if that is the way modern house design is heading, then we're all for it.

FACT FILE

Name: Tim and Ceridwen Coulson
Area: Monmouthshire
Build type: Self-builld
Size: 300m²

Build date: May 2010–May 11
House cost: £360,000
Build cost: £740,000
Cost/m²: £2,466
House value: £1.5m

CONTACTS

Architect Hall + Bednarczyk (01291 627777)
Main contractor MacCormac Construction (01873 851712)
Services engineer Building Energy Partnership (07710 724992)
Planning consultant DLP Planning Consultants (dlpconsultants.co.uk)
Windows Velfac (01536 313552)
Glazing system Fineline Aluminium (01934 429922)
Kitchen Harvey Jones (0117 923 8641)
Kitchen island Onnen Furniture (07957 136093)

Steel frame Morgans of Usk (01291 672253)
Zinc roof Rheinzink (01276 686725)
Temperature-sensitive rooflight Glazing Vision (0333 800 0881)
Bathroom tiles Mandarin Stone (01600 715444)
Sanitaryware Duravit (0845 500 7787)
Pocket doors Eclisse (0845 481 1977)
Heat pump NIBE (0845 095 1200)
Off-mains drainage Klargester (01296 633000)

FLOORPLAN

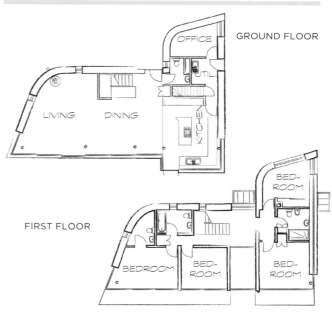

The house has been designed to make the most of views and maximise the potential for passive solar gain. The living and dining areas on the open plan ground floor are separated from the kitchen by a double-height 'slit' section, with full-height glazing allowing natural light to flood the interior. Upstairs, three of the four bedrooms – which are modest in size due to planning restrictions – enjoy far-reaching views.

Modern Makeover

Deborah Wilks has built on the best aspects of her Thirties Modernist bungalow to create a stylish 21st-century home

WORDS: JASON ORME
PHOTOGRAPHY: SIMON MAXWELL

Situated in an interesting settlement of a couple of dozen Bauhaus-style bungalows, built by the River Hamble in Hampshire in the Thirties by the tea impresario Sir Thomas Lipton, the home of Deborah Wilks is a classic example of how homes that are past their best can not only be restored but improved beyond all imagination. A gleaming white rendered example of sleek design born at the height of Modernism, when Deborah and her partner took it on it was all faded glory and not much else.

"We knew all about the potential with these very interesting homes," explains Deborah, who had previously remodelled another home on the same estate. "This one came with a brilliant site, with lawns down to the river front and views over the marina. It was well past its best and the layout was very cluttered, but the basics were there to be worked with, rather than totally ripped out. We wanted to emphasise the original design and bring it into the 21st century."

Over the years, the five bedroom bungalow had been stretched and pulled in various directions with the best of intentions, but perhaps not the best of design guidance. Deborah knew the value of expertise in this situation and called in Lesley Hally, from LA Hally Architects, to come up with a scheme that would be part restoration, part remodel, part opening up. "The 191m² house was actually quite dark, so the priority was to introduce space, light and airiness," explains Deborah.

The scheme that Lesley came up with was to remove many of the existing internal walls, including the main ones separating out the hallway, to create a largely open plan rear to the house including a kitchen, living and dining space. A home office is partially separated with a half-wall and the number of bedrooms has been reduced from five poky spaces to three larger rooms of a size more accommodating of things like en suites and large wardrobes. There are new windows throughout, and to the rear a suite of new openings, including bi-fold aluminium doors (from Smart Systems) and a feature circular window in the home office that is used, imaginatively, to provide a curved window seat. Most glamorously of all, the large roof terrace (the bungalow has a flat roof) has

been restored to its original majesty and now provides a huge party area complete with built-in speakers and a groovy, Saturday-afternoons-sipping cocktails-waving-at-passers-by vibe.

"The project itself was fairly stress-free," says Deborah, who co-owns a health club. "The architects had their own in-house project management service, so they dealt with the main contractors. We effectively rebuilt much of the front elevation and the whole of the roof structure has been rebuilt with added insulation. We were involved in most of the product choices, and obviously took on the interiors. The new heating system uses trench radiators – we considered underfloor heating but it didn't work from a budget point of view. Unfortunately the bespoke grid

covering, designed to tie in with the rest of the flooring (as opposed to the usual off-the-shelf brass models) ended up costing almost as much as an underfloor heating system anyway."

Walking round on a sunny late summer's day, it's difficult not to see the appeal here. The house is superbly open and crisp in its approach, and as a model of Modernism it's hard to beat, with a series of very-well-chosen pieces of art and furniture to blast out of all that white. The exterior, with a new through-coloured K Rend render gleaming in the brightness, looks brilliantly individual, with the roof terrace being a real highlight. "We're delighted with how it turned out," says Deborah. "We've massively improved the original, got what we wanted but also

The ground floor is warmed with trench heating, consisting of radiators placed in trenches around the perimeter. Large sliding doors open out to the garden

A charming circular window seat in the home office allows a framed view, as well as greater connection with the outdoors

been true to the style of the house. Some 80 years on, this project bookends the Modern era – we still love the exteriors, and with internal improvements, it is a very appealing combination."

The Bauhaus movement in the Twenties and Thirties is in many ways where Modernism really started. Established by architect Walter Gropius in Germany, it attempted to combine a single vision for the visual arts of painting, sculpture and, of course, architecture. The architectural style (Bauhaus means 'House for Building', which is the name of the school that gave the movement its name) rejected ornament and tried to capture the essence of Classicism in its most simple form. Essentials include the use of strong colours (white and grey being key) along with bold, often geometric lines.

FACT FILE

Name: Deborah Wilks
Area: Hampshire
Build type: Contempory extension and remodel
Size: 191m²

Build date: July 2012–Feb 13
House cost: £425,000
Build cost: £450,000
Cost/m²: £2,356
House value: £1.25m

CONTACTS

Designer LA Hally Architect (023 8061 6698)
Structural engineer RJ Watkinson (rjwatkinson.co.uk)
Sanitaryware, floor and wall tiles Porcelanosa (porcelanosa.com)
Kitchen Knightwood Kitchens (no longer trading)
External doors and windows Smarts Systems (smartsystems.co.uk)

External render K Rend (028 2826 0766)
Woodburning stove Saey Fenix flatline 90 (saey.com)
Inset floor radiator and mini canal trench radiator JAGA (jaga.co.uk)
Inset curtain rail Goelst (goelstuk.com)
Flooring Blueridge Flooring (blueridgeflooring.co.uk)

FLOORPLAN

In order to maximise the living space, the formerly five bedroom bungalow has been reconfigured and opened up in order to provide luxurious light-filled open plan accommodation. Now there are three large bedrooms which all benefit from en suites – the master also features a walk-in dressing area. External stairs lead to a roof terrace, which provides the perfect spot for entertaining.

Landscape Design

Melissa Brooks and James Warner's new home is designed to have minimal impact on its beautiful and secluded site within Dartmoor National Park

WORDS: DEBBIE JEFFERY PHOTOGRAPHY: NIGEL RIGDEN

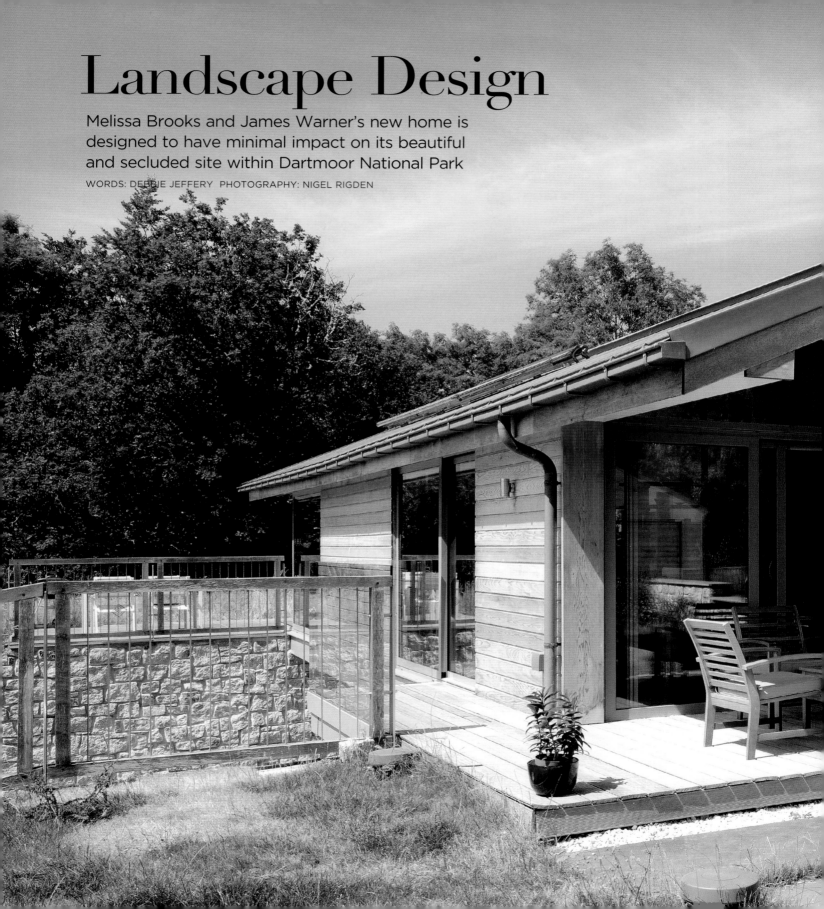

At entrance level, the house appears to be single storey — the rear reveals a different view, with a lower ground floor housing the bedrooms, which is built into the hillside. A decked seating area is sheltered beneath the oversailing roof. Granite walling lends an air of solidity to the moorland home

Standing on an elevated site, the new house
has been partially buried into the hillside and
is framed with granite-clad walls to reduce its
impact. The garden – previously a muddy field –
now features a small pond and cultivated lawn

Open Plan Living

The open plan living, kitchen and dining space at entrance level is divided into zones thanks to the clever placing of furniture. Corner sliding doors (from Olsen UK) in the dining area open completely to the raised terrace, creating an indoor/outdoor feel during meal times, while glazing in the living space continues James and Melissa's moorland views

Melissa Brooks and her husband, James Warner, didn't have far to travel when they left their much-loved family home to move into the brand new house they had built in their garden – but the two properties could not be more different from one another. One is a rambling Edwardian country pile, complete with associated draughts, endless maintenance and sky-high bills. The other is a compact, contemporary and energy-efficient new build which has been sunk into the hillside to ensure minimal visual impact.

The couple moved from their home in the Cotswolds to live in Devon 22 years ago, purchasing Gledswood House which stands in 13 acres of fields and woodland on the north-eastern edge of Dartmoor. "It was a wonderful family home, but very expensive to run," recalls Melissa. "When our daughter, Chloe, left home we really needed to scale down to somewhere more manageable, but leaving the area simply wasn't an option."

Fortunately, a solution was close at hand in the form of a small, run-down Thirties bungalow which stood in the grounds of the couple's home. Originally built for the gardener, this property had been rented out in recent years which meant that a planning submission for a replacement dwelling within Dartmoor National Park could legitimately be made.

The couple approached local architect Annie Martin, whom they had known since she was a girl. Impressed by Annie's other award-winning projects, Melissa and James met with her to discuss their brief for a more modestly scaled, contemporary home, which would feel both open and light.

"We're in our sixties now, and needed somewhere smaller and easier to maintain, with large windows, good access to outdoor space and plenty of storage," explains Melissa of the couple's wishes. "Fitting into the environment was absolutely key, and Annie had great vision and really brought together all of our ideas into one fantastic design."

The open plan kitchen benefits from a separate pantry and utility room. Cabinets were designed and made by Ben Huggins, including a large central island with an oak counter and plinth-level lighting

Melissa has a large collection of books, housed in a purpose-made, double-sided oak bookcase that wraps around the living area

It was essential that any proposal should be sensitive to the surrounding landscape, while embracing the tranquil country views from the elevated site. Lengthy negotiations with Dartmoor National Park followed – which included employing a planning consultant and producing artist's impressions – and planning permission for a replacement dwelling was granted in May 2010.

A detailed tender package was then created and a main contractor appointed to undertake the project through a JCT Minor Works Contract. Annie Martin took on the role of contract administrator, working closely with James, Melissa and the contractors.

Access to the rural site along narrow lanes proved awkward, however, for large vehicles, and the builder encountered rock during the extensive excavation process – as well as enduring harsh weather conditions while building on the moor through the winter months.

Beautifully crafted, the suspended steel staircase is clad in oak and appears to float up to the entrance level

Considered design

The design of James and Melissa's new home was inspired by the natural contours of their site, which was previously part of a field and attracts a multitude of wildlife and birds. The sloping ground adjacent to the new house remains unchanged, giving the opportunity to conceal the building, and a gravel track branching off the existing drive follows the contour of the sloping ground.

From the parking and drop-off point, the house appears to be a single storey building reminiscent of a discreet agricultural barn. Untreated cedar-clad walls help to reduce its visual impact and the simple, pre-weathered zinc roof echoes the grey shades of local granite and slate which feature so prominently in the design.

The entrance and sliding glazed doors to the south-east are set back to provide weather protection and to further reduce the apparent weight of the top floor. A granite-walled cloakroom defines the entrance, and grounds the building by linking it to the granite-clad retaining walls below. These two sloping retaining walls enclose a levelled grass area, and allow the lower ground floor bedrooms and study to enjoy easy access to the garden. The walls also provide a clear division between the cultivated lawned area and the surrounding landscape, which has been retained as natural grassland.

The largely glazed façade of the lower ground floor is set back by a metre to the south-west to provide solar shading and to lessen its visual impact. The house is obscured from the north-east by trees and connects completely with its moorland setting.

Bedrooms and bathrooms on the ground floor are mainly below ground level, and this element of the house was constructed with concrete and blockwork retaining walls. In contrast, the top floor living space was formed with a more lightweight steel and timber frame.

Many of the materials have been chosen for their durability and sustainable nature: low-maintenance aluminium windows and sliding doors from Olsen UK, granite stone walling, a zinc roof and sustainably sourced cedar cladding. Both structural and cladding materials (excluding the zinc roof) were non-specialist and could be completed by the main contractor, which was beneficial to both the build time and the budget.

A host of energy-saving and generating measures have also been introduced to the house. The roof and timber frame walls are heavily insulated beyond Building Regulations requirements, and as the lower ground floor is predominantly underground, the temperature is regulated all year round with the fully glazed south-west façade bringing in natural light, solar gain and ventilation. As the ground floor is cantilevered over the lower ground floor glazing, this provides shading for the bedrooms during high summer, and helps keep the rooms feeling cool and inviting.

A mechanical ventilation heat recovery system introduces clean, warm air throughout the house, and the underfloor heating and hot

water are fed by a 1,000-litre cylinder which is heated by either the woodburning stove, air-source heat pump or roof-mounted hot water solar panels, depending on outside conditions. Water for the property is provided via a borehole (with ultraviolet treatment), foul drainage is taken to a new septic tank on site, and surface water from the roof is collected and used for the WCs, dishwasher and washing machine.

"We did a lot of research into these technologies," states Melissa. "Our old house was heated by an expensive oil-fired Aga, which we don't miss at all because this house is just so warm."

It's all a far cry from Melissa and James' previous high-maintenance home. "It was always going to be a difficult house to leave, and I was adamant that I would only move into the new house if I really loved it," concludes Melissa. It is testament to Annie Martin's thoughtful design that, despite their high expectations, the couple are now happily ensconced in their newly completed home, and sent a note to her stating: "We wanted to thank you from the bottom of our hearts for creating this truly gorgeous home for us. We so love it."

FACT FILE

Name: Melissa Brooks and James Warner
Area: Devon
Build type: Self-build
Size: 240m²

Build date: July 2011–Dec 12
Land cost: £200,000
Build cost: £500,000
Cost/m²: £2,083
House value: £850,000

CONTACTS

Architect Annie Martin (anniemartin.co.uk 01647 272839)
Builder RM Builders & Contractors (01822 610509)
Consulting engineer John Grimes Partnership (01752 690533)
Landscaping Green Earth Landscape (01803 866635)
Kitchen and bookcase Ben Huggins (newbritishdesign.com)
Underfloor heating Continental (0845 108 7001)
Tiles Amtico (amtico.com)
Sanitaryware Ideal Standard (01482 346461)
Lighting Amos Lighting (01392 677030)
Air-source heat pump Danfoss (danfoss.com)

Blinds Inside Spaces (01395 222525)
Heat store Akvaterm (akvaterm.fi)
Zinc roof Rheinzink (01276 686725)
Sliding doors and windows Olsen UK (01777 874510)
Solar panels Viessmann (01952 675000)
Solar panels, air-source heat pump and heat store installation Atlantic Renewable Energy (01548 857768)
Ventilation and heat recovery system Nuaire (029 2088 5911)
Aquatherm woodburner Stoves Online (0845 226 5754)
Boiling water tap Zip Heaters (UK) (0845 600 5005)

FLOORPLAN

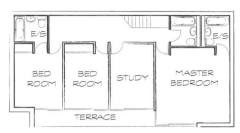

LOWER GROUND FLOOR

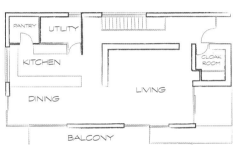

GROUND FLOOR

This new home has been built into its hillside setting and in order to make the most of its loch views, the open plan living accommodation has been placed on the top floor, including the master bedroom which benefits from an en suite with separate WC and dressing area. Thanks to the use of wrap-around glazing, all of the loch-facing rooms on the ground floor open out on to external terraces. The lower ground floor houses the guest accommodation and utility room.

The first floor appears to float above the predominately glazed ground floor – concealed steelwork was key in creating this contemporary façade. Cedar cladding, sourced from Vincent Timber, and black painted cladding differentiate the two floors. The cladding also works to disguise the juncture between the old and new structures

A New Era

Natasha Marshall and Neil Fullerton
have transformed a semi-derelict
commercial building into a light-
filled contemporary home

WORDS: CAROLINE EDNIE PHOTOGRAPHY: ANDREW LEE

Kitchen
The spacious kitchen diner enjoys views out over the garden through large sliding doors. "The ground floor is so open plan, we wanted the kitchen to look more like furniture, to blend in," adds Neil. "We chose a SieMatic design – the first company in the Sixties to create handle-less kitchens"

Natasha Marshall and Neil Fullerton's ambition to fashion a new family home from a tricky semi-derelict commercial building, located on a small back lane surrounded by the stately Victorian and Edwardian sandstone tenements of Glasgow's West End, was ambitious, but not foolhardy. Indeed, to prepare for the challenges of renovating this 'difficult' building – with its origins in the 1840s and with a hotch-potch of Sixties additions to boot – the couple actually cut their teeth on a similar conversion of a 19th-century commercial building, that's now their workplace, and located not too far from their new home.

"We learned a lot from the previous experience, which involved rebuilding and renovating a derelict printworks at the back of a city block," explains Neil, who managed both projects alongside Natasha and architect friends Stuart Cameron and Miranda Webster of Glasgow-based Cameron Webster Architects. "Both projects were similar in that they had tight lane access, which creates logistical challenges," says Neil.

The origins of Neil and Natasha's new home go back 15 years. "We lived in a flat opposite the lane for 13 years and we always said that if it came on the market we'd have to buy it," explains Natasha. "The original building was here before the tenements were built – the title deeds date from the 1840s. The previous occupant was an antiques restorer and there was also office space that we nearly rented out around 15 years ago."

A 'For Sale' sign went up in April 2010. "We opened the curtains in the sitting room one morning and saw the sign and phoned up right there and then," says Natasha. Following a chat with the sellers and planners, outlining their intention to convert the commercial property into a home, the couple eventually submitted a bid that was accepted.

One particular issue to address with the planners was providing adequate parking for this urban home. "Part of receiving planning permission required us to demonstrate that we could approach the main street, in forward gear, not in reverse," says Natasha. "If we had committed the whole courtyard to parking we could have done a three-point turn, but we were also keen to have a garden. The turntable, which is steel with nylon rollers, allowed us to have a garden and separate driveway. You drive the car onto it and when you're ready to go out you spin the car round by hand. The kids in the neighbourhood love it!"

An indoor-outdoor connection has been created via floor-to-ceiling glazing and the dark-stained external timber cladding which continues inside. The clever staircase appears to be cantilevered, due to a glazed balustrade, and timber used for the flooring is continued on the stair treads

Dark timber cladding hides a WC and two storage cupboards)

Clerestory windows and roof glazing ensure that the cosy living room is filled with natural light, without compromising privacy. The focal point of this room is the Stuv woodburning stove. "We love how it can be an open fire or log burner and looks stunning on the poured concrete hearth," says Neil. "And it's very low maintenance"

A good start was augmented by the fact that the building – which consisted of ground-level workshops and various upper-level timber office extensions – was in a good state of repair. "It was immaculate inside; the beams and concrete roof were sound. There were no maintenance issues… at that point," says Neil. A less-appealing aspect of the project was that it was a very dark building.

Bringing inside as much light as possible was the couple's main aim, but in order to do so, some major structural decisions had to be made. Essentially, the front section of the roof was taken away and the two interior walls and wall at the rear of the building had to be removed to insert windows. At one point only the two side walls and three quarters of the roof remained.

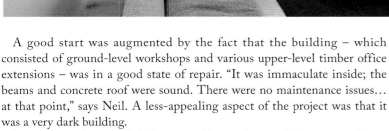

The couple's love of sailing inspired the teak details in the main bathroom. "We got the idea of the window louvres from a hotel that we were staying in, in the British Virgin Islands, where louvres next to the shower looked out to the sea," says Natasha. The exterior louvres also lend privacy to the bedrooms

However, the extensive structural work was well worth it – light now floods into the interior. "There are rooflights at the top of the building so when you walk upstairs you're looking up at the sky, which is a lovely effect," says Natasha. "And a slot has also been created in the middle of the living room so that there is always light. The little slot windows don't look as though they are doing a lot, but they're south facing so they bring in a lot of light for their size. These ended up being very expensive windows but definitely worth it in the end."

The first floor window louvres not only chime with the design, but they also have a very practical function. "Due to the fact that the tenements are so close we had to find a way of having a shower or bath with nobody seeing in. They are angled so that the surrounding flats can't see into the bathroom or bedrooms," says Natasha.

The resulting four-bed home is arranged over three levels, with an upper-level loft living area and roof terrace. The clever floating effect of the first and upper floor extension over the glass panelled ground level has been achieved by a steel span across the length of the building tied to the two existing boundary walls. "There is effectively a steel frame inside the new structure," says Neil, who visited the site regularly, hopping between work and the couple's nearby rental accommodation (they had sold their flat to raise funds for the build). "As well as the steel beam there are steel supports in the stair wall and in the corner where the utility room is located. The supports are cleverly concealed, which creates a real flow about the space."

The unusual cedar-clad upper extension connects cleverly to the ribbon-like black timber cladding on the ground floor. Aesthetically its effect is dramatic, but the design emerged from more practical considerations. "The shape of the front façade really hides what lies behind: the juncture between the new and existing structure," explains Neil. "The choice of the random cedar cladding and black painted timber, as well as the idea of the outside continuing inside – in this case the exterior shed going all the way through the house to form the main hallway – was inspired by some of the new buildings we saw during a trip to New Zealand."

The interior achieves a perfect balance between being both modern and soft. Natasha and Neil run a design studio in Glasgow, creating fabric ranges for various interior brands in the UK and Europe that sell into the interior industry worldwide. They designed all the fabrics in the house and had them specially recoloured to create "a soft palette that is really relaxing", explains Natasha.

In harmony with this soft, relaxing raison d'être are interior details such as the simple concrete slab fireplace, stove and log store, wide engineered whitewashed oak floorboards atop the underfloor heating and a clever lighting scheme. "The whole house is really relaxing," concludes Natasha. "You can't believe you're in Glasgow's busy West End, you don't hear a thing – it's like a little oasis."

FACT FILE

Name: Natasha Marshall and Neil Fullerton
Area: Glasgow
Build type: Self-builld
Size: 300m²

Build date: Mar 2009–Apr 13
House cost: £360,000
Build cost: £740,000
Cost/m²: £2,466
House value: £900,000

CONTACTS

Architect Cameron Webster Architects (cameronwebster.com; 0141 330 9898)
Stove Stuv 21 Stirling Stove Centre (stirlingstovecentre.co.uk)
Flooring Surface Plus (Glasgow) (surfaceplus.co.uk)
Siematic Kitchen Riverside Kitchens Glasgow (riversidekitchens.co.uk)
Windows Guardian Systems

Stirling (guardiansystems.co.uk)
Underfloor heating Mmaxx Glasgow (mmaxx.com)
Cladding Vincent Timber (vincenttimber.co.uk)
Bathroom and downstairs tiles Marazzi Tiles CTD (marazzi.it/en; ctdtiles.co.uk)
Fabrics Natasha Marshall (natashamarshall.co.uk)

At the very beginning of the project, with a long way to go....

"The aims were to transform a semi-derelict workshop and office building into a calm, private city house. The dark, damp building was turned into a light, contemporary home for our clients, who wanted to stay living and working in the West End of Glasgow"

FLOORPLAN

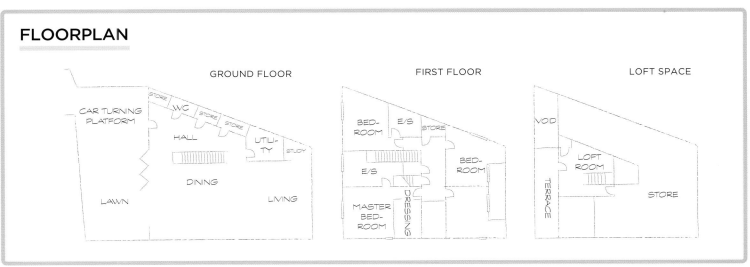

GROUND FLOOR

CAR TURNING PLATFORM
STORE
WC
STORE
STORE
HALL
UTILITY
STUDY
DINING
LAWN
LIVING

FIRST FLOOR

BED-ROOM
E/S
STORE
E/S
BED-ROOM
MASTER BED-ROOM
DRESSING

LOFT SPACE

VOID
LOFT ROOM
TERRACE
STORE

Around the Corner

Adam Glabay and Shauna O'Handley have built a contemporary cedar-clad house – utilising every inch of a tight corner plot adjoining a Victorian terraced street

WORDS: ALEXANDRA PRATT PHOTOGRAPHY: NIGEL RIGDEN

Terrace
Aluminium folding sliding glass doors (from Kloeber) feature in the kitchen and dining space and open this entire corner of the house to the sheltered terrace beyond

Walk along the typical Victorian street where Adam Glabay and his wife Shauna O'Handley now live and their new home is not difficult to spot. Situated at the end of a row of terrace houses in South London, this new timber house – which contrasts dramatically with its more traditional brick-built neighbours – wraps itself around the corner to maximise the tight, triangular-shaped plot.

Not only is the contemporary structure clad vertically in cedar, but its curved, sculptural design and lack of visible windows along the south façade has led passers-by to question whether the building is even a house at all. "Some people did wonder if it was going to be a public building at first," says Adam of the couple's new home.

As native Canadians, both Shauna and Adam grew up in homes built by their parents, and were familiar with the idea of self-build. "It's pretty common in Canada, and when we came to the UK more than 10 years ago, we renovated several one bedroom flats before

deciding that we wanted to build our own house," Shauna explains. "We'd been looking online and saw a couple of other London plots with planning permission in the same price range, but this was our favourite."

After purchasing the plot, the couple sold their flat in North London and moved to live with friends during the 11-month build. "I have to admit that our lack of experience made the whole process pretty terrifying," says Adam, who works as a computer programmer.

Given that timber buildings are widespread in Canada, the couple decided that their new home would be timber framed. "We looked at having a factory-built frame but struggled to find a builder who would erect it, so we ended up having it stick-built on site," continues Adam. "Our builder was recommended by the architect, and they managed the project between them – although we got more involved as the build progressed."

Once the highly insulated timber frame was complete, it was then clad externally with untreated cedar, impregnated with fire retardant

Open Plan Living and Dining Room
Underfloor heating has been installed beneath engineered oak flooring throughout the open plan ground floor, which overlooks the rear terrace. Adam and Shauna crafted some items of furniture themselves, including the dining table

An awkward plot

Shauna and Adam met with their neighbours at a street party two years before building work started on site – and kept in constant contact during the project, which helped to maintain a good relationship with all concerned. Despite its unusual appearance, and the fact that the structure adjoins what was previously an end-of-terrace property, the neighbours' reactions were surprisingly positive.

"Our house steps down, so it's lower than the others, and the majority of the windows face on to the internal garden which is around one metre below pavement level, so we're pretty private and don't overlook anyone," explains Adam. "It was quite a challenging design for first-time self-builders, and having a good team of people to support us was critical."

Originally the site of two lock-up garages, the urban infill plot had already been granted planning permission for a highly contemporary house, which appealed to Adam and Shauna. "It really makes the most of the tiny scrap of land and takes its cues from the characteristics of the plot with its angles and curves," says Adam. "We purchased the plot with an approved design in place by architect Nagan Johnson and retained Red Squirrel Architects to implement it and make any subsequent changes."

Excavating the site to lower the new house created footings reminiscent of a muddy swimming pool filled with rain, and the side wall of the neighbouring house needed to be underpinned to avoid the possibility of subsidence. A raft was constructed over concrete strip foundations, which were engineered to accommodate the clay soil, and a steel frame was erected to support part of the new structure.

"Choosing a considerate and respectful builder was important because we were building so close to other homes, and we were really lucky to have such a great contractor because we didn't want to fall out with any of our new neighbours," says Shauna.

Some disruption was caused by building on the junction of two roads, and working on such a small site brought specific problems regarding access and storing materials. But, overall, the build ran smoothly and was carefully coordinated by the contractor.

"It wasn't an obvious plot of land to build on, but in many ways the constraints have helped to shape the house," explains Adam. "As a result, we don't have any standard-shaped rooms – and we even used full-sized paper cut-outs of beds to make sure everything would fit – but for us, it's all part of the charm."

Sleek, handle-free wardrobes were built by the contractor in the master bedroom and painted a caramel colour to contrast with the dark blue feature wall

and then fixed to battens. "We wanted the timber to fade and silver so that it would mellow into the plot," explains Adam.

"The planted roof was a condition of planning and of our lender, the Ecology Building Society, who only lend on properties and projects that respect the environment," recalls Shauna. "The lower kitchen roof is visible from one of the bedrooms above, and the wildflower sedum mix means that we have small, multi-coloured flowers growing up out of the green sedum.

"To be honest, we weren't familiar with the Ecology Building Society prior to purchasing the plot, but we met their criteria and we achieved the U values they recommend," she continues. "We installed underfloor heating on the ground floor, with radiators in the upstairs rooms because we wanted to be able to heat bedrooms quickly for short periods of time." Other eco credentials incorporated into the house include energy-efficient triple glazing (which also restricts the passage of sound), LED lighting and grey water recycling for flushing the toilets.

The interiors are a particular highlight, offering sleek contemporary

Rising up from the open plan living and dining room, the bespoke staircase was designed by the architect and built with square-edged oak treads together with a simple glass balustrade

The fuss-free, minimalist kitchen has no handles and neutral dark grey-painted doors, so the room's colour scheme may be easily changed in the future

furnishings within an open plan arrangement. Engineered oak flooring has been laid over underfloor heating in the kitchen, living and dining room. This space overlooks the sheltered outdoor courtyard through two sets of folding sliding glass doors – flooding the space with natural light. These open the entire rear corner of the house to the decked terrace beyond, which effectively becomes another room when the weather allows.

"We relied heavily on the professionals to get the house watertight, but then we wanted to be more involved in the fun aesthetic things like the flooring, sanitaryware, light fittings and the kitchen, which we supplied," says Adam. "Some of this came from eBay, and we actually made items of furniture ourselves to save money – including the dining table and beds. We probably exceeded our original budget by around 10 per cent, but we kind of expected that anyway."

The original deadline of July 2012 came and went, but the couple moved into the completed house just a few weeks later. "There's not too much we'd do differently in hindsight because we had such a good team, and we're very pleased with the outcome," says Shauna. "We kept looking at the rooms and thinking they would be too small – of course, they were fine once everything was completed and plastered."

Our favourite part of the house changes during the day depending on where the light is, but overall we love the main living and dining area – which was structured so that there are distinct zones within the open plan space. The niches on the south elevation are also a favourite feature, with aluminium copings at the top that finish everything off.

"Despite being fairly well organised and doing plenty of research before the build, we were still surprised by the number of decisions that needed to be made. We would definitely consider building again though, because we've really enjoyed the process and now we know what to look out for in the future."

FLOORPLAN

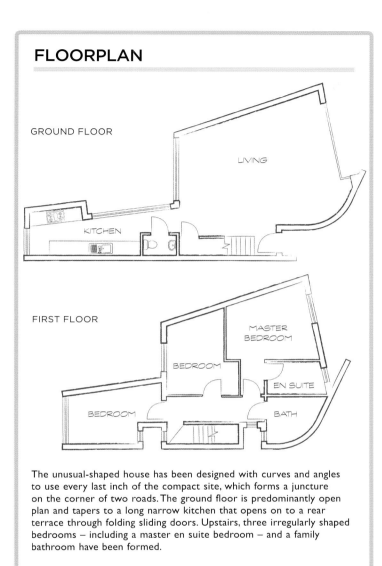

GROUND FLOOR

LIVING

KITCHEN

FIRST FLOOR

MASTER BEDROOM

BEDROOM

EN SUITE

BEDROOM

BATH

The unusual-shaped house has been designed with curves and angles to use every last inch of the compact site, which forms a juncture on the corner of two roads. The ground floor is predominantly open plan and tapers to a long narrow kitchen that opens on to a rear terrace through folding sliding doors. Upstairs, three irregularly shaped bedrooms – including a master en suite bedroom – and a family bathroom have been formed.

FACT FILE

Name: Adam Glabay and Shauna O'Handley
Area: London
Build type: Self-build
Size: 100m²

Build date: Nov 2011–Sept 12
Land cost: Undisclosed
Build cost: £350,000
House value: £700,000–£1m

CONTACTS

Original architect Nagan Johnson (020 7633 0200)
Project architect Red Squirrel Architects (020 8699 6766)
Building contractor PI & Co (07971 605926)
Structural engineer McHenry Structures (mchenrystructures.com)
Geotechnical survey Ground and Water Ltd (0333 600 1221)
Lender Ecology Building Society (0845 674 5566)
Windows Velfac (01223 897100)
Aluminium folding sliding doors Kloeber (01487 740044)
Roofing company Southern Counties Roofing Contractors (01245 241333)
Warranty provider NHBC (0844 633 1000)
Waste connection EJ Taylor & Sons Ltd (01621 828661)
Grey water recycling Aquaco (01892 506851)
Kitchen units Coloro Ltd (01942 717839)
Staircase balustrade Glass London Ltd (020 7635 8000)
Carpentry Scott Firth (020 7732 9145)
En suite shower screen Spiral

Hardware Ltd (01842 811818)
Engineered oak flooring Jordan Wood Floor Warehouse (020 8684 3056)
Dining table legs Franz Faust Linoleumprodukte (Germany) (08841 625617)
Dining table top and bookcase materials Whitten Timber (020 7732 3804)
Matt white mosaic tiles Walls and Floors (020 8788 5900)
Blue glass mosaic tiles Tile Supply Ltd (0843 2894 230)
Recessed LED lighting Online Lighting (0800 046 9041)
Pendant and exterior lighting Wayfair (0800 169 0423)
En suite shower heads Taps Empire (01708 874955)
Taps/traps/kitchen sink QS Supplies Ltd (0116 251 0051)
Aluminium downpipes Rainclear Systems Ltd (0800 644 4426)
Soft-close kitchen drawers, LED strip lighting and bedside flex reading lights M&D Components (01964 650865)
Kitchen appliances AO.com (0844 324 9222)

"Once you find people you're happy to work with, you need to give them a certain amount of autonomy – nobody wants someone breathing down their neck the whole time. By the end of the build we probably did become quite annoying!"

When Old Met New

Simon Shaw and Giuliana Cortese have restored a
period cottage, adding a contemporary extension which
not only provides much-needed family space, but
continues the narrative of this historic home

WORDS: JANE CRITTENDEN PHOTOGRAPHY: ALISTAIR NICHOLLS

Rear Elevation
This extension sits upon six oak legs and is constructed from a stick-built timber frame, in homage to the original cottage

WHEN OLD MET NEW

Simon Shaw and Giuliana Cortese's restoration and extension of a Grade II listed cottage is an inspiring example of how contemporary architecture can sit comfortably with the historic to create a fabulous 21st century family home. However, the ingenuity of the design is also in how it acknowledges the architectural story that began way back in 1650 when the cottage was built.

"We resisted the temptation to finish everything off perfectly – it's otherwise hard to read the story of the house," reflects Simon, who trained as an architect and designed the extension himself. "So, we've left areas of the original structure visible for people to see how the cottage was constructed."

The family's new home has a fearlessly modern rear extension, but it has been designed to enhance the historical architecture of the 17th century cottage. While there is a clear differntiation between the two parts of the building, the transition is harmonised by a glass-ceilinged bridge.

"This is a visual link that connects and defines the old and the new, but also introduces much-needed light into the heart of the home," Simon adds. The glass on the ceiling and walls surrounding the steps provide a visual and physical connection between the old cottage and the new extension. This contemporary steel bridge has subtle references to Simon's favourite architect, Carlo Scarpa, who designed the entrance bridge to the Fondazione Querini Stampalia museum in Venice

The couple bought their cottage in July 2008 after deciding to move out of London with their daughter Francesca (and Scarlett-Grace who was due later that year). They liked the easy pace of life in this village just outside Thame, and the cottage was a good size with four bedrooms and a Fifties extension.

The interiors had not been updated for some 30-odd years and the Grade II listed cottage was also in a Conservation Area, but this didn't put them off. "I felt I could make a design statement here as the organisation of space, the scale and the volume were all good to work with," Simon reflects.

Simon was so keen on the project that he developed plans for a

Kitchen/Dining Area
The polished concrete floor and exposed steelwork provide a modern industrial style

The two-storey, flat-roofed extension was built on the same level as the cottage – the sloping site required excavating – and so is barely visible from the street (below left). Expansive glazing introduces light and provides views over the landscaped gardens; a triple-glazed, Swedish window system minimises heat loss (top and bottom right). A glazed link connects the old part of the building with the new (above left), and offers glimpses of the neighbouring Grade II-listed church

WHEN OLD MET NEW

Parts of the cottage wall have been exposed (see right-hand wall) to reveal the original fabric of timber frame, wychert and stonework; the finish is lime plaster applied during the renovations. The new extension's timber frame has been sympathetically left on show too

The generous first-floor ceiling heights were a big selling point. In the master bedroom, a partial wall divide has been added to create the en suite. The original roof trusses at the junction between the cottage and new extension (traditionally covered in lime plaster) have been exposed

The living room has all the markings of a cosy country cottage, with its exposed beams and inglenook fireplace. The walls were stripped back to the original stone grumblings, and replastered with breathable lime to prevent damp

contemporary extension before the sale had completed – and very little has changed along the way.

"We only had £150,000 to spend, so I had everything planned out and all the hard decisions made before we began," he says. "It was better this way as there were minimal changes on site."

But living in the cottage to begin with was not an entirely comfortable experience. The existing extension was constructed in a single skin – it leaked heat, and was damp and cold. The cottage too was damp. The ancient wychert walls – a traditional material similar to cob, made from a mix of white clay and straw, and local to Buckinghamshire – had been plastered over with a synthetic coating, meaning moisture had become trapped within the fabric of the building.

It was a slow room-by-room start, with Simon juggling the restoration work with his full-time job as a creative director for a global communications agency. Evenings and weekends were spent stripping back the walls and reinstating them with lime plaster and a lime finish that would allow them to retain heat as well as breathe.

During this time, Simon also had a pre-planning meeting with the local planner and historic buildings officer to show them his 3D model of the two storey, contemporary rear extension. "I talked about the ethos behind how the building would work for us as a family rather than focus on how the building was going to look, and they were both very receptive," he reflects.

In October 2009, Simon submitted his planning application but the planning officer he'd been dealing with went on long-term leave. It wasn't until March 2010 that his documents could be reviewed, but there were still more delays to overcome (read page 73 for more).

It was January 2011 when the Fifties extension was finally knocked down. But then, levelling the site – to accommodate the two storey addition – proved more problematic than anticipated.

"Although the site was on a slight slope, I didn't realise how much top soil we'd need to dig out, and it cost about £500 per load," Simon

Ikea kitchen units have been dressed with marble and stone worktops: the units were taken apart to strengthen them in order to support the new, heavyweight tops, which now appear to float above the units

explains. "As a result, the groundworks for the house and garden ended up being about 20 per cent of our budget."

The extension was constructed in timber frame using the stick-build method, whereby the frame is put together on site by hand. "I wanted it to be built as a contemporary version of the cottage's timber frame," says Simon, "but it was also easier to reconcile the wonky cottage walls by building this way."

The extension was designed to be an energy-efficient shell – unlike its leaky predecessor – with Kingspan insulation used internally and woodwool insulation boards on the exterior. Triple glazing was also specified to trap solar heat which is, in turn, distributed around the house through a heat-recovery ventilation system.

The entire project took 15 months to complete with Simon helping project manage and finishing works such as the tiling, decorating and some second fix joinery.

Although the project took longer than anticipated, Simon was pragmatic. "Quality, money and speed are the three things you've got to play with when you do a building project," he says. "My builders

were brilliant and I didn't want to compromise their quality; I didn't have any more money either so I had to be flexible about the time it took to complete.

"We now have the best of both worlds living here," Simon continues. "We have the best of modern living and entertaining in our new extension, and the beauty and character of the historic cottage where we retreat to in the evenings."

Simon and Giuliana's resulting home also represents the next chapter in the architectural story of the village. Indeed, the judges of Aylesbury Vale District Council's 2012 design awards were so impressed with the project, that it received a Highly Commended award and Simon was praised for his empathy. "This, above everything else, is what I am most pleased about," says Simon.

"They said my scheme had a narrative and that was exactly what I wanted to achieve. Every piece of architecture has a story to tell and I wanted to introduce a narrative to our historic cottage with its new contemporary extension, so people who come here understand how the building was put together."

FLOORPLAN

GROUND FLOOR

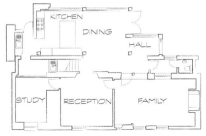

FIRST FLOOR

The ground floor of the new extension is largely given over to an open-plan kitchen/dining room where direct access to the garden is provided via expansive glass doors.

The existing cottage contains a cosy living room, a study and a further reception room. The new extension also features a family bathroom and bedroom, which is linked to three bedrooms (including the en suite master) within the existing cottage via a steel bridge.

FACT FILE

Name: Simon Shaw and Giuliana Cortese
Area: Buckinghamshire
Build type: Renovation and extension
Size: 185m²

Build date: Feb 2011–May 12
House cost: £470,000
Build cost: £150,000
Cost/m²: £811
Total cost: £620,000
House value: £750,000

CONTACTS

Architect Simon Shaw of Beam Cottage Architects (beam-cottage-architect.com)
Main contractor Building Envelope Evolution (buildingenvelope.co.uk)
Garden construction Agripower (01494 866776)
Bridge steelwork DSM Fabrication (01296 623099)
Windows Tansums Fönster (0115 932 1013)
Doors Earthwood (07912 158762)

Balustrades Seagul Balustrades (01215 250020)
Shelving Vitsoe (020 7428 1606) Elfa (aplaceforeverything.co.uk)
Bathrooms Bathstore (bathstore.com)
Worktops Marble Workshop (01844 296096)
Flooring Bolon Flooring (bolon.com)
Sleepers and decking UK Sleepers (01604 862261)
Roofing RoofKrete (roofkrete.co.uk)

Design and planning

The Grade II listed cottage was built in 1650 and is at the end of a row of terraces next to the Grade II* listed village church. It was surprisingly spacious for a cottage, with four bedrooms arranged off one long corridor. However, very small utility spaces – including a tiny shower room and a small kitchen – were not suited to family life. Simon saw great potential in the property. "Upstairs had good head height instead of low beams, so I knew if I introduced light into the building, it would feel airy," he says. "I felt I could reorganise the space and add a new extension too."

Simon identified five key areas of change in his scheme: 1. Demolish the single storey Fifties brick and block rear extension that was of poor build quality; 2. Build a two storey, contemporary rear extension for a family kitchen/diner, utility and entrance hall on the ground floor, and bedroom and family bathroom on the upper floor; 3. Create a glass link to join the old and new buildings and introduce light; 4. Restore the original fabric of the historic cottage to make it dry and warm; 5. Reconfigure the layout of the cottage to allow for a bigger living area downstairs and an en suite to the master bedroom upstairs.

Simon was keen to pay homage to the historic spot, so although the extension is four times as large as the old Fifties extension, he ensured the design was proportional to the size of the original property and garden.

"The new bedroom is only 3.2m deep, and the extension is set away from the neighbours to protect their light. It is also stepped back from the drive to avoid adverse views from the street."

The extension is built into the sloping site with a flat roof – made from RoofKrete, a maintenance-free, waterproof membrane – so the height doesn't exceed the ridge height of the original property.

When the couple's planning permission and Listed Building Consent was finally looked at in March 2010, the planning and historic buildings officers were supportive of the new extension. However, the Parish Council remained focused on the roof – and misconceptions over flat roofs leaking.

The couple's application had to go to the county planning committee meeting. "I distributed documentation prior to the meeting, explaining the technical detail of the project and focused my speech on why the future of the village depended on the need for family homes," he says. "I explained that if I wasn't given permission, this property would remain a big cottage for two retired people – and you can't just have retired folk living in a village."

Simon and Giuliana's application won unanimous support from the committee in August 2010.

Living Space
Fixed glazing is a major feature of
this home, while sliding doors from
Harmony Profiles allow spectacular
views over the estuary

Full Throttle

Michael and Angela Nathenson's new home in Salcombe is
a fine example of the great results that can happen when
you approach a self-build project with a bit of gusto

WORDS: JASON ORME PHOTOGRAPHY: NIGEL RIGDEN

A sunken courtyard garden acts as both a lightwell and source of stylish greenery to be enjoyed from the interiors as well as outside

FULL THROTTLE

Kitchen
The Bulthaup kitchen has a smart, twin-island layout with Gaggenau and Miele appliances

The master bedroom makes the most of views out to the estuary, thanks to the sliding doors' minimal frames

Michael Nathenson is not a man lacking in drive or energy. At the age of 70, he looks about 20 years younger and has approached the building of Mew Stone East – a striking contemporary home on a sloping site in Salcombe, Devon (complete with dreamy views of the estuary) – in the same way that he seems to have approached things for the past half-century or so: full throttle, burn to empty, not so much no-holds-barred as all-holds-encouraged – and then some.

At 50, having worked all across the world in educational systems, including helping to establish the Open University (which is when he left his native USA for the UK), he decided to change professions and make something of his life-long interest in architecture and design.

Teaching himself CAD, he began to take on run-down properties in Hampstead and Belsize Park and turn them, quite lucratively, into brilliant homes. Part designer, part developer, part force of nature, his property development business, Unique Environments, is responsible for creating spectacular projects across North London that draw on his international design tastes for the top end of the market.

"I was using builders from the Salcombe area who would drive up to London on Sunday night and come back on Thursday night," begins Michael. "They wanted somewhere to show off what they were doing to their friends and family, and my wife Angela and I were looking for somewhere by the sea to move to. Salcombe seemed the perfect spot to satisfy everyone.

"We found something going through auction – an old pink bungalow sitting on a 0.4-acre site. To make it work financially (this being Salcombe, the plot ended up going for £1m), we knew that we would have to build two houses in its place – given the high-quality specification that I insist on. So the plan was set – we would build two properties side-by-side and sell off one to enable us to live in the other." Planning permission was achieved with constraints limited to requiring a fairly conventional gable end and a restriction on ridge height.

Michael is not a man to tinker around the edges. The scheme required total domination of the site – heavily sloping down to the street level, it needed excavation beyond most measures. In the end, some 2,000 tonnes of rock were dug away for the houses, with the vast majority reused on the site for the vast front wall, side walls, terraces and complex street-edge structure, which now consists of garaging and an ingenious custom-designed lift. It's undoubtedly impressive – indeed about the only thing that you might have actually expected is the story of the build, which (hardly surprising considering Michael's wealth of experience and access to tradespeople) was a masterclass in project management.

A conventional blockwork and render construction, the house is designed around large elements of glazing, both fixed and flexible,

prioritising the view over the estuary and Natural Trust land. Living spaces are on the upper floor, while bedrooms and office spaces sit below – although, cleverly, Michael has ensured the main entrance to the house is at middle level.

Internally, the finishes are exquisite, and feature a Bulthaup kitchen with Miele and Gaggenau appliances, elegant, wide-planked white oak engineered flooring (Michael insists on it after years of problems with solid wooden boards), and some fantastic design features, including a sliding electric rooflight (from Natralight) that can be opened by remote control and automatically closed thanks to a rain sensor. But, it is the overall feel that is the most successful element – a kind of Australian/Californian mix that, thanks to the large amounts of natural light, feels quite different to the contemporary homes we see elsewhere.

One of the key reasons for this is the landscaping scheme, which is an exercise in ambition. While most self-builders would have spent a few years trying to manipulate and tame the site, Michael took an 'in for a penny, in for a pound' approach, with every single square inch of the site landscaped to perfection. The cascading design, on many levels – incorporating terraces, zones and all manner of level changes – is an undoubted highlight and really encapsulates his approach to the whole scheme – brave and innovative.

"I wanted to incorporate a range of planting from Tuscany," he says. "But when I checked out the price of using a local UK importer, I thought I could do it better myself. I researched Italian suppliers and ended up going direct to a supplier in Pistoia in Tuscany. We ended up with two massive truck loads turning up on site direct from Italy and it cost a third of the price."

The resulting house is a huge achievement, mixing the very best in interior design with a bold, contemporary exterior look and first-rate landscaping. Benefitting from a spectacular site with great views, Michael and Angela have created something very special here which, despite the undoubted professional approach, offers some valuable lessons for the amateur self-builder, not least in terms of project management. "Organisation is the absolute key to success," says Michael. Yet this house, for all its scale and above-average build cost, also shows the importance of taking control of the site, and imposing your plans through sheer strength of will. Energy can get you a long way, as Michael has proven.

FLOORPLAN

GROUND FLOOR

FIRST FLOOR

Mew Stone East makes the most of its estuary views by placing the living accommodation on the top floor, which boasts an open plan kitchen diner stepping down to a large living area and terrace. The middle floor houses an en suite guest bedroom with courtyard, and the master suite, complete with dressing area, en suite and terrace. The lower floor (not shown) includes three bedrooms (two en suite), a family bathroom and laundry.

FACT FILE

Name: Michael and Angela Nathenson
Area: Devon
Build type: Self-build
Size: 370m²

Build date: 2007–2012
Land cost: £500,000
Build cost: £1m
Cost/m²: £2,702
House value: £2.95m

CONTACTS

Design and build Unique Environments (01548 844944)
Sliding doors and windows Harmony Profiles (01392 202295)
Bulthaup kitchen, Gaggenau and Miele appliances Kitchen Architecture (01865 426990)
Bathroom fittings CP Hart (0845 873 1121)
Limestone bathroom flooring Mandarin Stone (01600 715444)
Limestone slabs for showers Contec (01726 71198)
Light fittings, switches and sockets CEF Electrical (cef.co.uk)
Ironmongery and entry door system Williams Ironmongery (01299 250824)
Electrically operated rooflight Natralight (01215 532300)
Underfloor heating Timoleon (01392 363605)
Internal doors Jason Pengelly Joinery (07853 266704)
Wardrobes Bedroom Ayes Furniture (07711 255134)
Fireplace West Country Fires (0844 748 0118)
Paint Farrow & Ball (farrow-ball.com)
Curtains Jam Interiors (01395 222525)
Engineered wood flooring The Solid Wood Flooring Company (01666 504014)
Landscaping slate Contec (01726 71198)
Kenmart Timber & Slate Products (01626 833564)

Modern Minimal

Colin and Anneka Cowan have built a new coastal home for their retirement based on minimalism, modernism and restraint

WORDS: DEBBIE JEFFERY PHOTOGRAPHY: NIGEL RIGDEN

A simple Scan woodburner was built into the wall, with log storage beneath

Staircase/Hallway

Stan Bolt designed the industrial-looking oak, steel and glass staircase, which stands on a plinth and is lit by natural light, courtesy of the strategically placed rooflight above

Living Room
Limestone flooring has been laid over underfloor heating throughout the open plan living space. Sliding glass doors may be opened to connect indoor and outdoor spaces

For Colin and Anneka Cowan, less is most definitely more. The couple dislike clutter and prefer pared-down, minimalist interiors that are easy to maintain – which is why their white sugar-cube of a self-build is their ultimate fantasy.

Perched high above the beach in Exmouth, on the east coast of Devon, their newly built four bedroom house replaces a rather clunky dormer bungalow which had been tweaked, extended and remodelled to within an inch of its life. Bedrooms had been added in the roof space and a new sunroom was built onto the back from which to enjoy the sea views, resulting in a mish-mash of clashing styles.

When Colin and Anneka first viewed the bungalow it was the location and sea views which thrilled them, however, and not the existing property. A side gate leads directly onto the coastal path, and as avid walkers who own three large dogs, the couple knew they would make good use of this access.

The Cowans had built two houses before, and wanted their third to be ultra-modern and of a more suitable scale for a retired couple with visiting children. In fact, their new home is a touch smaller than the house it replaces

"We wanted to build just one more house – a home beside the sea for our retirement – and when we discovered Exmouth we selected an area of just six houses which we liked," recalls Anneka. "The home search company we were using sent out letters to the owners and discovered that the one house we preferred was coming onto the market. We literally picked the location rather than waiting for something to come to us – and it worked."

Pared-Back Palette of White
"Stan's suggestion for rendered interior walls was something we weren't initially sure about, but are very pleased with. All these walls also have rounded corners and no skirting or architraves," states Colin

The orientation of large areas of glazing maximises the benefits of passive solar heating, and the use of masonry walling and stone flooring creates an energy-efficient heat sink

St Laurence House is bold in concept and form yet modest in scale. It has been positioned further back on its site, ten metres away from the original bungalow, creating a more generous rear garden facing the sea

No planning permission existed for the plot, but the Cowans remained undeterred. "We've renovated several properties in the past and had previously built a house in the US and another in Cornwall, so the prospect of demolishing the existing bungalow and starting from scratch wasn't too daunting," explains Colin.

Finding the right architect for the project proved straightforward, thanks to an article the couple had read some years before about a house designed by award-winning architect Stan Bolt, whose practice has developed a reputation for imaginative, site-specific work – generally within the south west but occasionally further afield and abroad. Bolt appreciates Thirties modernism, and his designs reflect this.

"We love ultra-modern architecture, and there was never any question that this was going to be a highly contemporary house," states Anneka. "We'd kept the article on one of Stan's houses in Salcombe, which was when we first saw his work, and as soon as we'd bought the bungalow in Exmouth we contacted Stan to design a replacement."

Two different design suggestions were produced for the prominent waterside site, based on the Cowans' brief. "We left the external look entirely up to Stan," says Colin, "but internally we knew the exact measurements of every room and the open plan layout we wanted, based on previous homes we've lived in. We have three children who visit, so three guest rooms were essential, and the utility/boot room

Minimal interference

St Laurence House replaces a far fussier dormer bungalow and responds directly to both the opportunities and constraints of its cliff-top site in Exmouth. Every detail has been carefully considered, working with a minimal palette of materials to create an effortlessly pared-down effect. A resin-bonded driveway leads to the large pivoting oak entrance door, which is a particular Stan Bolt trademark. Inside, an unobstructed vista directly through the house to the glazed rear elevation culminates in spectacular, far-reaching coastal views through aluminium-framed glass doors.

"The spaces have an inside-outside quality, marrying the interior with the environment," says Stan Bolt. "A straightforward approach to construction reduced unnecessary details, and produced an inherently durable building that functions efficiently and will age gracefully."

White was definitely the order of the day, and white sanitaryware and kitchen units stand against white walls. The effect is softened by the limestone flooring which runs throughout the downstairs rooms, with engineered oak flooring upstairs. Splashes of unexpected colour bring the spaces to life and prevent them from feeling austere.

Electrically-operated blinds have been fitted, and are virtually invisible when open to leave glazing unobstructed. "In many ways the build has been an exercise in trying to conceal as much as possible," says Anneka. "It's all very simply done and there isn't an inch of space that's not used."

was something we had in the States and it's now the perfect place for our dogs to clean off after we've been walking on the beach."

Initially Colin and Anneka favoured the more adventurous of Stan's two designs, which consisted of two staggered blocks of accommodation, but later they decided that the simpler, less dramatic option would give them the interior layout they wanted. Interestingly, the new house is smaller than the existing five-bedroom bungalow it replaces.

"Most people try to build something larger when they replace an old house, but there are only two of us here and we wanted a more modest home," explains Anneka. "We refined our homes over the years until now we've got it just right. We made a few tweaks to the design, such as moving the position of the kitchen so that it creates an L-shape, but overall we loved Stan's ideas and the planning process was pretty straightforward."

Anneka and Colin sold their home in Bath and went to live in their Cornish holiday home during the build, which began in September 2009. "We were up and down to visit the site quite a bit, and our architect managed the build for us," says Colin. "The weather was a big problem and the rain caused delays in the autumn, with snow at Christmas, so the build took longer than we'd originally thought. But moving in was the best feeling!"

Extensive structural steelwork supports large areas of glazing, inset into rendered blockwork walls, and the materials were carefully selected to withstand the vagaries of a marine setting. The result is unadorned and makes a strong statement, whilst engaging sympathetically with its environment. "We don't feel as though we've downsized because the house is so light and open," says Colin. "And we know we'll never tire of the view."

FLOORPLAN

GROUND FLOOR

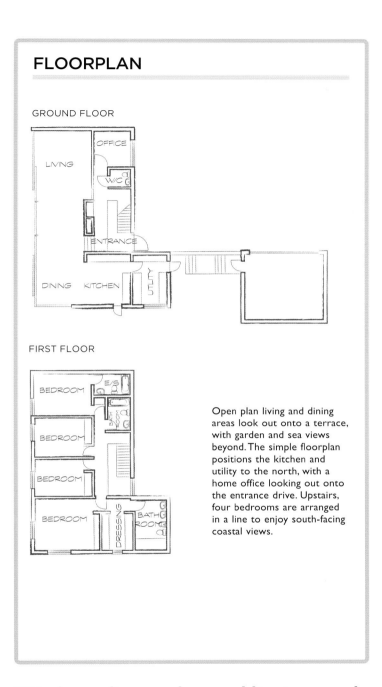

FIRST FLOOR

Open plan living and dining areas look out onto a terrace, with garden and sea views beyond. The simple floorplan positions the kitchen and utility to the north, with a home office looking out onto the entrance drive. Upstairs, four bedrooms are arranged in a line to enjoy south-facing coastal views.

"We love ultra-modern architecture, and there was never any question that this was going to be a highly contemporary house"

FACT FILE

Name: Colin and Anneka Cowan
Area: Devon
Build type: Self-build
Size: 295m²
Build date: Oct 2009–Sept 10

Land cost: Undisclosed
Build cost: £394,000
Cost/m²: £1,335
House value: £1.75m

CONTACTS

Architect Stan Bolt (01803 852588; stanboltarchitect.com)
Structural engineer Nicholls Basker Partners (01626 776121)
Building contractor Imperial Construction (01392 361777)
Rooflights and minimal windows sliding-door systems I-Q Glass (01923 218348)
Windows Sapa Aluminium (01684 853500)
Roofing RoofKrete (07970 455050)
Precast concrete cills and copings Mexboro Concrete (01803 558025)
Lintels Stressline

(01455 272457)
Stove Scan (scan.dk)
Internal doors Premdor (0844 209 0008)
Kitchen and utility units Ikea (ikea.com)
Worktop Corian (dupont.com)
D-line ironmongery Allgood (020 7387 9951)
Underfloor heating Wavin (0844 856 5152)
Garage door Garador (01935 443722)
Shower fittings Ideal Standard (01482 346461)
Slate flooring Kenmart (01626 833564)

Low Profile

After visiting some 100 plots and properties, then dealing with unusual planning constraints, Ian McLean and Robbie Pancic have finally created a self-built home that ticks all their boxes

WORDS: JANE CRITTENDEN PHOTOGRAPHY: ALISTAIR NICHOLLS

Roof Line

The low-profile, unobtrusive flat roof was an important aspect of the design — it allows for uninterrupted views of the loch from the nearby road. Originally intended to be a green roof, budget constraints meant the specification was changed to gravel instead

Living Accommodation

The house's timber ceiling joists are exposed to allow for a line of rooflights in the centre of the house. They mark a differentiation between the two flat-roof heights but, more importantly, they draw valuable south and south-west light into the main living area. The floor-to-ceiling windows (from Marshall Brown) capture a pretty picture-perfect view of the loch – providing the ultimate in spectacular art for the room. Underfloor heating has been laid under the polished concrete floor and is supplemented with a woodburner from Danish firm, Morsø

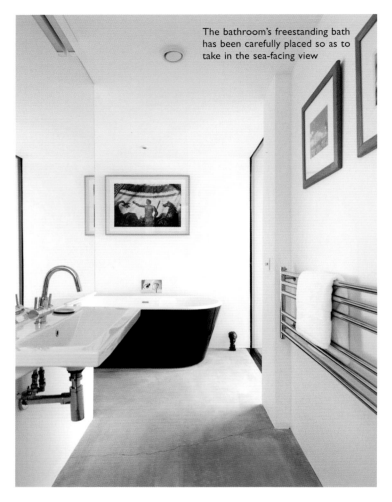

The bathroom's freestanding bath has been carefully placed so as to take in the sea-facing view

Ian McLean and Robbie Pancic's low-lying home on the Isle of Skye is almost hidden in the rugged landscape – merely offering a suggestion of a roof line to anyone who might happen to be passing nearby. The home's flat roof, simple elevations, and grey stone and larch cladding are all so subtle that the eye is instead drawn over the top to soak up the views of Loch Dunvegan beyond.

It was this stunning outlook that sold the site to Ian and Robbie, who are now in the very enviable position of being able to enjoy the island's scenery every day. But finding this idyllic spot took determination. "We wanted somewhere rural and close to the sea with an uninterrupted view, and we didn't want to compromise!" explains Ian of their ideal location. "We looked at more than 100 plots and houses to renovate. Quite often we'd find the ideal spot and then discover there was planning permission directly in front or

to the side for another house, which wasn't any good."

Ian and Robbie began their search in early 2011 after falling in love with the Isle of Skye while on holiday. They were ready for a change of pace in their lives, and resigned from their respective jobs in England with a dream of finding enough land to start a horticultural business or market garden, and to build a holiday let alongside their own new contemporary home.

After searching all over the island, fate intervened when they drove past open croft land in Galtrigill one day and saw the spectacular view, after which they made some enquiries about the land through their solicitor.

"We found out that the owner was living in the croft house on the 15 acres of land, but was potentially interested in selling." The wheels for the sale were barely in motion when Ian and Robbie started looking for an architect to design their new home. They had already

Rooflights bring much-needed natural light into the kitchen (situated at the windowless rear of the property)

Scottish crofts

Historically, crofts were parcels of agricultural land on estates that crofters farmed on behalf of the wealthy landowners. The crofters were tenants, but were entitled to pass the tenancy down through their families.

Today, croft houses and land can be sold, but there are conditions that have to be met under the Crofting Reform (Scotland) Act 2010, such as ensuring crofts carry on contributing to the development of rural areas. This doesn't necessarily mean that crofting has to be a full-scale farming business: crofters grow fruit and vegetables or go into forestry and woodland management, and it is common for crofters to have another job that provides their main income.

Crofts are found mainly in the Scottish Highlands and Islands, and are regulated by the Crofting Commission which agrees any change of tenancy or ownership. They take into account local crofting demands and whether the proposed owner intends to live and work on the croft and how they'll contribute to the local community.

For Ian and Robbie, the crofting law was in their favour. A croft is entitled to a croft house (so the tenant/owner can work the land) and since they bought their land without a croft house, they had good reason to build one. Ian says he and Robbie were quite anxious about how they were going to deal with the crofting law, but they got a good solicitor who did all the paperwork for them.

"Buying the croft became a new adventure for us that we would never have imagined doing three years ago," says Ian. "But we were excited about the whole avenue of opportunity and are busy planning for our market garden, hens and ducks, and this year we'll be getting some sheep."

decided to use a local firm and were drawn towards Dualchas Architects' modern designs, which they'd seen around the island. "We were really excited by what Dualchas could do in terms of contemporary design using traditional materials, but also with how their houses fit so well into the landscape here," Ian explains.

As the view across the loch was the clincher for Ian and Robbie, it was only natural that they would want to build a sea-facing house with a wall of glass. But they were unsure whether this was going to be physically or even financially possible with the stormy weather that can so often lash across the island.

"We were delighted when Dualchas said they could build a steel structure for the windows at the front and use super low-E insulated glass," says Ian. "They also had the clever idea of running a line of glass along the back of the house between the two roof heights which brings in lots of south and south-west light."

However, the design still needed to convince the planners. Although the top of the croft was inside the Settlement Development Area (SDA), Ian and Robbie's preferred location for their new home was just outside.

A pre-planning meeting on site was arranged and Dualchas Architects were able to highlight an area where the gradient falls and the house could be built into a natural overhang. Furthermore, the design would feature a single storey and a flat roof, so the house wouldn't obstruct the views from the road.

The planners were in agreement and approved Ian and Robbie's application in November 2011; but it wasn't until the following summer that work got underway.

"The tenders came back 50–100 per cent more expensive than we were expecting, so it was a big disappointment," says Ian. "We thought we'd have to rip the plans up and start afresh, but instead we took out one of the bedrooms and reduced the size of all of the other rooms."

Initially, Ian and Robbie had hoped to build for £180,000 but reluctantly agreed on a build contract for around £70,000 more. They chose a builder known to the architects who they could trust, and were impressed with their work ethic and 'can-do' attitude. Understandably, with no steady income, the pair were very cautious with their budget. So they were dismayed when just days into the project the groundworkers hit extremely hard rock while digging the foundations — adding an extra four weeks to the build schedule and around £10,000 to the already-stretched budget.

Things began to improve once the structure was up, however, and at the end of 2012 building work started on the holiday house, too. A few months before the main house build got underway, Ian and Robbie had sought planning permission to build a holiday home on their land. "We felt we needed a multiple income source to make it sustainable for us to live here," Ian explains, "so we decided to build a second property that met the expectations of today's modern traveller."

The local authority were in favour of the plans that would encourage tourism to the area and supplement Ian and Robbie's croft livelihood; they were also happy with the design for the new holiday home.

The mono-pitched roof and corrugated aluminium façade of the holiday home presents a modern take on the old agricultural buildings that can be seen dotted around the countryside on the Isle of Skye – with the surprise of a contemporary wall of glass so guests can enjoy the view just as much as Ian and Robbie do.

Although Ian and Robbie were on site every day, busily setting up the infrastructure of the croft for their new market garden, their lack of building experience made them nervous about getting too involved with either this project or the build of the main house.

"In hindsight, we should've appointed a project manager," Ian explains. "We didn't always know what conversations had gone on between the architect and the builder, and with one focusing on design and the other on building, we think an impartial project

manager could've made sure our needs were met too."

The house was completed in 11 months, with Ian and Robbie ready to move into their new home in June 2013. Despite some frustrations along the way, they're delighted with how the house has turned out. "This project was always about getting the right location, so we're really pleased we invested in these fantastic floor-to-ceiling windows," says Ian on reflection. "The view is absolutely stunning; we see the weather rolling in and we see amazing wildlife, so we're really getting everything we can out of living here."

FLOORPLAN

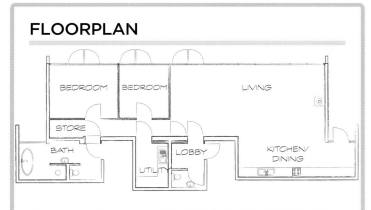

BEDROOM

BEDROOM

LIVING

STORE

BATH

LOBBY

KITCHEN/
DINING

UTILITY

The simple, single storey layout has been arranged so that the main accommodation is orientated to face the loch and to make the most of the views through the full-height glazing. An open plan living, kitchen and dining area occupy one half of the home, while two bedrooms, a large bathroom, storage space and a utility are sited at the opposite end of the house.

FACT FILE

Name: Ian McLean and Robbie Pancic
Area: Isle of Skye
Build type: Self-build
Size: 110m²

Build date: July 2012–Jun 13
Land cost: Undisclosed
Build cost: £260,000
Cost/m²: £2,364
House value: Unknown

CONTACTS

Architects Dualchas Architects (dualchas.com 01471 833300)
Builders James MacQueen (skyebuilder.co.uk 01478 640292)
Bath Royce Morgan (roycemorgan.co.uk 0845 116 1616)
Kitchen John Lewis

(johnlewis.com)
Woodburner Morsø (morso.co.uk)
Pavers Terram (terram.com 01621 874200)
Windows Marshall Brown (marshall-brown.co.uk 0141 563 5000)

Ian and Robbie's holiday home sits on their crofting land, and its floor-to-ceiling glazing makes the most of views over the loch

The low-lying house is designed to sit snug and blend into the landscape without obstructing views from the road. Windows to the front look seawards towards Loch Dunvegan, the Western Isles and the Outer Hebrides

"We wanted somewhere rural and close to the sea with an uninterrupted view, and we didn't want to compromise! We looked at more than 100 plots and houses to renovate"

Doubling Up

Wayne and Lorrie Bilsborrow have transformed their granite farmhouse with the addition of a contemporary timber extension

WORDS: CAROLINE EDNIE   PHOTOGRAPHY: NIGEL RIGDEN

Set in 89 acres of rolling Aberdeenshire farmland, this home combines the original 19th century granite farmhouse with a large, contemporary-style, larch-clad extension. The extension is constructed in 150mm stud timber frame, filled with phenolic QUINN-therm insulation

When Wayne and Lorrie Bilsborrow were looking for an opportunity to create a new home in rural Aberdeenshire, they had in mind: "A few acres, a nice setting, and a house to enjoy our retirement," according to Wayne. What they have, rather spectacularly, ended up with is 89 acres of rolling farmland with panoramic views, a fishery, and following a recent extension and renovation project, a new home featuring a canny combination of a traditional 19th century granite farmhouse with a contemporary larch and stainless steel extension. The result is Bogindhu – a 21st century steading.

The Bilsborrows, who have lived and worked in the Aberdeenshire area for the past 24 years, first saw and then immediately bought the Bogindhu site and farmhouse at the very end of 2004. "We liked the position of the house as it was well away from any road. The big plus was also the panoramic views," says Wayne. Although, as Wayne also explains: "At the time we bought the house it wasn't what we were looking for as a home, but that wasn't important because it was always in our mind that whatever we bought we would probably change to meet our own requirements. We lived in the existing house a year before we began any work, deciding what to do next – we wanted to get a feel for the place."

During this process of 'rumination', the Bilsborrows worked out a wishlist for the redevelopment of their farmhouse. "I wanted the new extension to be contemporary – I like the look of metal roofs and timber cladding. The main thing I wanted was for it to be different from the granite house," explains Lorrie. "I also wanted to be able to look at the views from my bath and to see the fisheries from the main living areas of the house. I was keen to have a big kitchen, a new en suite bedroom in addition to the three bedrooms in the granite house, as well as an office and a sitting room downstairs that could be used as an additional en suite bedroom to accommodate my mother."

"And I don't like doors!" adds Wayne, who is originally from Canada and admits that doors are not a big feature in Canadian houses. "I like the feeling of open space, so we were keen to have a double-height space in the living area. Above all, we wanted to take advantage of the views and introduce as much light as

The vertical larch boarding will fade to grey with age and cost a touch over £25,000. The roof is ArcelorMittal terne-coated stainless steel (the brand name is Uginox), while the expansive windows from Velfac take in the glorious views

Kitchen
Located in the renovated farmhouse and featuring units from Drumoak Kitchens and Fisher & Paykel appliances, the kitchen is a pointer to the rustic heritage of the house

possible, hence all the windows going down to the floor."

Navigating through the couple's wishlist was the job of architect David Wilson of Aberdeenshire-based Room Architects, who is also the couple's son-in-law.

"I saw the redevelopment of Bogindhu as a modern interpretation of traditional farm buildings," explains David. "I was keen to create a welcoming farm court to the entrance side of the building, closely following the pattern of the farmhouse and steading. It was with this in mind that the L-shaped arrangement of the house was developed. The form and materials of the new building are direct references to traditional, Aberdeenshire agricultural buildings; a simple pitched roof finished in profiled stainless steel sits above vertical larch boards, whilst the stainless steel band running round the building is reminiscent of the flashings and covers found over barn doors. The link, consisting mostly of glass, forms both the entrance

and acts as a visual separation between the old and new elements." The project also involved re-instating and re-pointing some of the granite details of the original farmhouse.

Internally, the volume of the new extension is double height in the living area, with open rafters adding drama to the design. A gallery overlooking this space and openings through to the link, as well as a stair crossing into the living space, all provide visual connections between the levels and adjoining spaces, while still maintaining the sense of 'rooms'. Overall, the house features five bedrooms, three bathrooms, a kitchen diner, a study and the main living space.

"Care was taken to differentiate the accommodation within the existing house and the new extension," explains David Wilson. "The bedrooms within the existing wing are smaller in scale to reflect the dimensions and proportions of the granite building while the rooms within the new addition are larger and more open, with window

DOUBLING UP

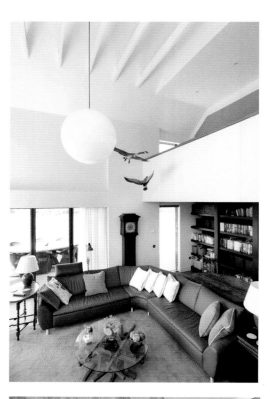

The link between the new timber frame structure and the existing farmhouse has become a glorious double-height space used as an informal sitting area, overlooked by a galleried landing

openings orientated to take advantage of set views."

The planning process was straightforward; the extension replaced an existing structure. The only change made was to replace the proposed zinc roof with a stainless steel one due to concerns that the run-off water from the larch cladding, which contains tannins, may have discoloured the zinc. This change didn't affect the budget though as the 0.4mm steel roof was the same price as the proposed 0.8mm zinc roof.

The 14-month construction, which went on site in autumn 2009, was also painless, save for one factor that was outside the control of the couple, their architect and their contractor – the weather.

"The construction did overrun, but we had one of the worst winters (2009) on record to contend with," explains Lorrie. "Work had to come to a standstill as there was two feet of snow around here. We were living in a static caravan on the site whilst the work was taking place and Wayne had to put straw three-bales-deep around the caravan to try and cut out the draught. It was fun!" laughs Lorrie. The cold spell also had a devastating effect on the newly installed underfloor heating.

Despite the weather delays and overruns, the project came in under budget. "There was provision in the contract to take account of variations," explains architect David Wilson. "There were extra things that we added in but we always knew what these extras were along the way – so there weren't any surprises at the end of the contract." And as

Lorrie explains, this was achieved by not having to make any major compromises. "In terms of the fixtures and finishes, we chose exactly what we wanted whether it cost a lot or not. We've mixed and matched the likes of the Ideal Standard sanitaryware and £110 Ikea kitchen sink with high-spec details such as the Hansgrohe mixer taps and showers."

At the top of the staircase is the open bridge between old and new Bogindhu, from where Lorrie describes seeing deer, otters and even an osprey. So rather unsurprisingly, she concludes that: "There's not a thing I would change about the house."

A bespoke highlight is the new, beautifully handcrafted staircase constructed by Hall & Tawse. It weighs around 3,000lbs, features 160 sheets of plywood, and was plastered in situ — it even had to be lifted in through the large window openings

FACT FILE

Name: Wayne and Lorrie
Bilsborrow
Area: Aberdeenshire
Build type: Farmhouse
renovation and extension
Size: 360m²

Build date: Sep 2009–Nov 10
House cost: £0 (already owned)
Build cost: £446,500)
Cost/m²: £1,239
House value: Unknown

CONTACTS

Architect Room Architects
(01224 443591 room-architects.
co.uk)
Quantity surveyor Murray
Montgomery (01224 633771)
Main contractor MCC Joinery
& Building Contractor
(01651 821182)

Windows Velfac (velfac.co.uk)
Sanitaryware Ideal Standard
(01482 346461)
Kitchen Drumoak Kitchens
(01330 811555)
Appliances Fisher & Paykel
(0845 066 2200)

Underfloor heating

The underfloor heating was important. "I didn't want radiators cluttering up the house," says Wayne. "So now the property benefits from underfloor heating, apart from the first floor of the original granite house.

"During construction, the system was tested with water and the water was left in. We then experienced -23 deg temperatures and the pipes all froze and burst, and all the floors had to be dug up. I think that people should be aware of this, as underfloor heating is so popular now. It's my belief that the system should be emptied, or anti freeze put in.

"The house was covered by insurance so this did not add any extra costs to the build contract, but the floor issue with the pipes bursting delayed us over three months," adds Wayne.

"One of the delays was losing the drying time when the floor had to be taken up," continues architect David Wilson. "To put floor tiles on top of a screed, there has to be five per cent moisture content and a concrete screed dries at 1mm per day. So if you've got 50mm then you need 50 days before you can put tiles down. The whole thing did not affect the contract, but it did delay the whole project."

"Above all, we wanted to take advantage of the views and introduce as much light as possible"

FLOORPLAN

An L-shaped floorplan has been created with the addition of the new extension. The original farmhouse now features an office and kitchen on the ground floor, with the extension providing scope for a double-height living room, boot room, garage and ground floor en suite bedroom. Upstairs there's a spacious en suite master bedroom while three further bedrooms share a bathroom in the existing granite farmhouse.

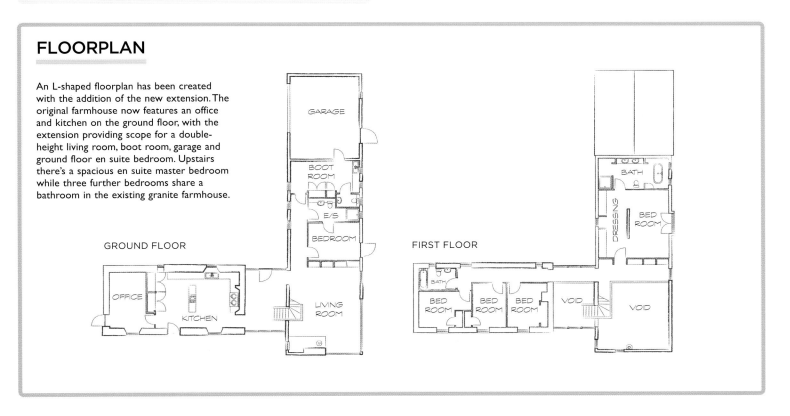

Geometry Lesson

Concrete and glass work in harmony to add architectural wow to what started out as an ordinary Seventies home, leaving a dynamic contemporary villa in its wake

WORDS: CAROLINE EDNIE PHOTOGRAPHY: DAVID BARBOUR

A two-storey red-brick property has been dramatically reimagined and transformed into a contemporary home. The house is clad in a combination of concrete-effect panels, made of reinforced cast resin, and white JUB render. The home has also been extended to accommodate a snug on the lower level as well as a viewing gallery on the upper level

GEOMETRY LESSON

According to project architect Alastair MacIntyre, the "sheer geometries" of his latest project – a remarkable home that recently emerged on a hillside on the eastern edge of Gare Loch in Argyll and Bute – meant that every detail had to be just right. These sheer geometries, however, don't even begin to describe the soaring cantilevered 'viewing pod', projecting out towards the sea and Arrochar Alps mountain range beyond. What's even more remarkable than its formal audaciousness and ambition is that the house actually started life as a Seventies red brick two storey home, which on first view reminded owners Alan and Linda of a community centre.

"We could see beyond the red brick," admits Linda, who like Alan was brought up in Scotland, but over the past 30 years have lived in locations ranging from Cheshire to Tokyo, Connecticut and London, due to Alan's work. "We've always thought of Scotland as home and have family here, so we spent our summers travelling around looking for potential locations for our permanent home."

When the red brick house went up for sale, the couple fortuitously met the son of the previous owner, whose childhood friend had spent a lot of time in the house as a teenager and was working in nearby Glasgow as an architect. Following the purchase of the house and its surrounding three acres, that childhood friend, Alastair MacIntyre, was invited by the couple to revisit and reimagine the house according to their vision for a light-filled, view-soaked house.

"We had strong ideas about the design elements," explains Alan of his visions for the new home. "We collected photos of features that we liked and wrote a design narrative beside these, saying 'we like this because...'" The couple's ideas were also influenced by their travels abroad, as Linda explains: "We wanted lots of light and textures – a modern house with a Japanese influence in its simplicity."

The design response, according to architect Alastair MacIntyre was radical. "The original house had a rigorous design profile in its own right – it was essentially two houses linked by a

While the reconfigured home effectively occupies the same footprint, the new cantilevered extension projects out to create an additional gallery and provides architectural interest to the rear façade, where contrasting building materials have been used to great effect

staircase. Having known the house, I knew its shortcomings. I knew we were looking for a slim-line form (which the original house had), clean lines and views towards the water from the main windows.

"The staircase was a weak link in the original house," continues Alastair, "so there was a great opportunity to open that up and create a fantastic entertainment and gallery space beyond the staircase which overlaps like a two storey link with a view. It is a signature feature of the house now, with a cinematic view of the sea and hills that you see as soon as you step inside the entrance door. Then other views open up as you come down the stairs." Essentially, Alastair has reimagined the house as: "Part Sixties Californian cantilevered concrete and glass John Lautner house; part *The Man Who Fell to Earth* – in the way that Alan travels round the globe yet he's fallen to earth on this

particular spot."

One of the house's main motifs is the unique concrete-effect rainscreen panels which were inspired by Frank Lloyd Wright's Los Angeles villas. These panels, which were designed to give some relief to the plainer exterior walls, were arrived at only after no small amount of material experimentation. "Concrete would have been too heavy so we had to devise a rainscreen that looked like concrete but was much lighter," says Alastair. "This is a technology by Capvond which we had not used before, with its simulated concrete panels manufactured using a 'reinforced cast resin system'."

Innovation is writ large in this element of the home, which is a striking addition to the mature gardens that surround it. However, on a more prosaic level the building effectively occupies the same footprint as the existing house, which is why

The high-spec Italian curvilinear kitchen (left) contrasts with the sharp lines of the home's exterior, while the long island with integrated appliances has been angled to face the glazed wall and dramatic views. In keeping with the exterior cladding materials, the home's interior adopts a neutral palette of white and grey. The large open plan living/dining space (above and opposite) is zoned by a central fireplace clad in the same concrete-effect panels as those used on the exterior, while a 'wall' of glazing allows the views to be fully appreciated

Thanks to the home's clever, reimagined design, a walkway from the entrance hall leads to the cantilevered extension which provides a gallery to enjoy the views; it also allows visitors to glimpse them upon entry

there was little in the way of planning issues. "The original carcass was there but the way it was going to look was entirely different," admits Alastair. "The only space added is the area of the new viewing pod." The original foundations were essentially retained but altered on the lower section of the lounge as this drops down a level. Underfloor heating has been installed here, while the upper section has been largely retained but relined and reinsulated, and the roof replaced with a single ply membrane.

The private spaces, such as the en suite bedrooms, have been arranged along the more private entrance wall on the upper level – which appears single storey from the front. "The bedrooms are inspired by living in Japan, where everything is very low and simple," says Linda. The amount of glazing in the bedrooms has been reduced to afford greater privacy too.

In stark contrast, the sea-facing façade of the main living areas features a Sky-Frame 'wall' of glazing set atop a white concrete perimeter walkway. "Not only does the walkway create an intermediate space between the garden and the house, it also reflects the light back into the house," explains Alastair. "The house benefits from reflected light from the loch, and also sunlight hits the loch and bounces up again, almost like a double-whammy effect. As a result the ceilings in the house are never dark." Another exterior device that has been continued in the living area is the central fireplace, which features an internal chimney constructed of the same Capvond concrete-effect panels that appear on the exterior.

Indeed, the detailing that project architect Alastair was keen to achieve has been realised throughout the house with a range of high-spec features, including bespoke chestnut doors that feature an abstract illustration of the home's floorplan in wood, created by the builder Allan Leckie. The Italian curvilinear Pedini kitchen and circular living area snug also adds a contrasting softness to the building's 'sheer geometries'.

The couple, who were living in their London

Floor-to-ceiling glazing on the lower level opens the interiors up to the stunning Gare Loch and Arrochar Alps beyond.

home during most of the build, also ensured that high-spec details were achieved by choosing not to scrimp on key features, such as the single-paned glass in the viewing pod, which could have been made up of two or three much cheaper panes. "We have an open mind and enjoy the same aesthetic approach as Alastair. He's been a real driver behind the design, so we were keen to support his ideas. It was great having someone who knew the previous owners and house, and in fact, the core design hasn't really changed since we first accepted the brief and it went into planning," says Alan.

"The challenge in a house like this is that you cannot be careless in the detailing," concludes Alastair. "It's a sheer and precise concept that you have to stick to rigorously and think about it all the way through."

FACT FILE

Name: Alan and Linda Raleigh
Area: Argyll and Bute
Build type: Contempory extension and remodel
Size: 426m²

Build date: Mar 2012–Jan 14
House cost: Unknown
Build cost: Unknown
Cost/m²: Unknown
House value: Unknown

CONTACTS

Architect McInnes Gardner Architects (0141 332 3841)
Structural engineer ATK Partnership (01475 787797)
Main contractor, plumbing, heating and doors Allan Leckie (07713 401863)
Render JUB (jubrenders.co.uk)
Roofing SRS Group (0141 551 9555)
Sky-Frame windows Gray & Dick Ltd (0141 952 9619)
Pedini kitchen and appliances Trevi Suppliers (020 8549 9990)
Flooring Parkwood (020 8878 6377)

Insulation Kingspan (kingspan.com)
Rainscreen panels Capvond . (0141 876 9000)
Garage doors Hörmann (01530 513000)
Bathrooms supplier Victor Paris (Glasgow) (0845 607 6944)
Master en suite sanitaryware Artelinea (artelinea.it)
Tiles Porcelenosa (porcelanosa.com/gb)
Strata (stratatiles.co.uk)
Surface Tiles (surfacetiles.com)
Interior design Annabel Bertie (bertiedesign.com)

The architect's view

The challenges of the site had been dealt with in the existing house, and the rigour of the design as it stepped down the hill had been addressed. Working with the existing footprint and foundations made sense and I always liked the way the house addressed the loch, so the opportunity was for its next evolution – reinterpreting the original design concept.

FLOORPLAN

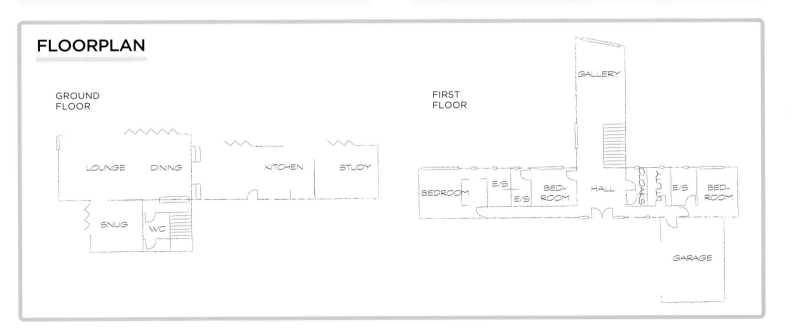

GROUND FLOOR

LOUNGE   DINING   KITCHEN   STUDY
SNUG   WC

FIRST FLOOR

GALLERY
BEDROOM   E/S   E/S   BED-ROOM   HALL   CLOAKS   UTILITY   E/S   BED-ROOM
GARAGE

Front Elevation
Making the most of its large plot, this former bungalow has had a radical remodel with a new first floor extension featuring twin gables. A palette of contemporary building materials clads the exterior; cedar and slate-effect cast concrete tiles break up the front elevation

Remodelled Retreat

Stuart and Elmarie Ward have created an
impressive contemporary family home on a budget
thanks to a radical rejig of their dated bungalow

As a developer, Stuart Ward was well-placed for knowing how to create amazing homes, so when he came across a Fifties bungalow on a large plot in east Dorset back in early 2013 he already had strong ideas as to how to transform the dated building into his and wife Elmarie's dream home.

"There are lots of bungalows on huge plots in this area and there's a lot of SSSIs (Sites of Special Scientific Interest), so not many of these large plots are allowed to be subdivided," explains Stuart. "When we viewed the bungalow we could see there was a substantial five-bed house next-door and that gave us an idea of what we could get away with and what would be appropriate for the area. The property cost us £310,000 and we knew we wanted something modern that we could afford. We were driven by economics – the idea of creating a dream house while getting the most out of what we already had here.

"The project was also my way of getting back in the saddle after being ill. I'd previously been asked to build a Tony Holt house in Poole for a client and despite having never taken on a new build I was keen to take up the challenge. Towards the end of the project, however, I fell ill with acute symptoms of chronic fatigue syndrome which left me exhausted and struggling to complete the most basic of tasks, so we decided the best solution here would be to extend."

With a clear idea in mind for the extension and remodelling of the old bungalow, Stuart approached architectural designer Tony Holt to help visualise his plans and turn them into a reality. "I had an idea of what I wanted and knew I was after something modern with twin gables. I also knew that in order for the project to be comfortable with the planners the house had to have a traditional element to its design as there were no contemporary houses on the road," explains Stuart. "I knew Tony from the Poole project and had seen a lot of his designs on his website which I liked, so I put together CAD and render drawings and then sent these to him."

Part of Stuart's brief was to try and keep the spaces as versatile as possible – for instance what is now the snug and open plan dining area could easily be swapped around. In order to maintain his healthy lifestyle, the brief also included a home gym. "We looked at what was already there and what we could and couldn't work with," says Stuart. "What is now the cinema and gym, however, was predetermined by the existing bungalow; the rest of the spaces on the ground floor which form part of the extension are more flexible. We wanted open plan areas but it was also important to plan in those quieter spaces to retire to in the evenings.

"The planners were pretty good," continues Stuart. "It's a unique build on a road with an eclectic mix of houses. The only issues we had were regarding the proposed ridge height, which we agreed to lower by half a metre. Our application was granted first time."

Work started on site in September 2013 with Stuart taking on the role of project manager and builder, and together with a local labourer, he began semi-demolishing the old bungalow to make way for the rear extension, along with removing the internal walls to open up the ground floor. Towards the end of digging the footings for the new extension, however, they suffered from heavy rainfall which caused the water table to rise – the works ground to a halt from the end of October right through to February 2014 as a consequence.

Once work was back underway, the build itself went quickly thanks to constructing the walls of the new extension in a single-skin of 240mm-thick aircrete blocks bonded together with adhesive. The bungalow was extended to the rear by approximately 3m and steel thrown up across the open plan space to open that section of the ground floor up, making the link between old and new seamless.

"This thin-joint construction technique is a brilliant way to build quickly and we imported the materials from Europe," says Stuart. "It was just myself and one other guy handling the building work. We could have done it quicker and perhaps cheaper by getting the professionals in, but for me this was like therapy and took my mind off my illness and gave me a focus without any pressure of getting the place built by a certain time – I could just take it easy."

In order to provide a contemporary exterior, a slate-effect cast concrete tile was chosen for the detailing. "Where we have elements like the front door we then used a cedar batten to add contrast. By using different textures it helps to break up the façade," says Stuart.

In total the project took around 18 months to complete, including the four months where the majority of the work was put on hold due to the rain. "Coming in from the on-site caravan every day and seeing the spaces come together really allowed us to see what did and didn't work – enabling us to make changes along the way if necessary. With doing it yourself you've got that ability to make changes, whereas if you're going through a team of contractors then changes can involve cost implications," says Stuart.

The house was completed in December 2014 – although as Stuart points out, a project is never truly finished – and what was once a tired

The designer's view

The existing bungalow was very cramped and failed to make the best use of the site. By adding a new storey this provided a cost-effective way of increasing the footprint of the building and the rear extension allowed for modern open plan living which breaks out on to the rear amenity space which is covered thanks to a roof overhang.

The design worked to retain elements of the bungalow to keep costs down while offering increased living accommodation. The external façade also underwent a contemporary facelift. The build cost Stuart achieved was just phenomenal – not many people could accomplish what he did. He even built the staircase and front door himself!

bungalow on a large plot with cramped accommodation has become a large contemporary dwelling which makes the most of its site thanks to an extensive remodel. Meeting the Wards' brief, the property has been opened up to the rear to feature a large open plan kitchen/dining/living space which now works well for entertaining and large family gatherings. Equally, the home offers private spaces too for when Stuart and Elmarie need some peace and quiet. Upon entry, the double-height hallway with galleried landing and staircase (built by Stuart) is also partially open plan to the rear, with a curved glass wall zoning the entrance space while allowing guests to flow through into the kitchen/diner and providing views out to the rear garden from the front door.

Open plan accommodation has also been introduced in the new master suite. "We saw the idea of the open plan bedroom and en suite in a hotel we visited," says Stuart. "As the new master bedroom was large we knew that this concept could easily be accommodated here. The slate-effect cast

concrete tile fireplace (the same material also used on the exterior, hallway and ground floor fireplace – creating a sense of continuity) adds character to the master suite and helps break up the bedroom and bathroom space. It's great to sit in the bath and be able to look through the fireplace and enjoy garden views over the balcony on the opposite side of the room, and glimpse the views further beyond that."

In order to bring light into the home, heavy doses of glazing have been added to the front and rear, with glazed gables to the new first floor, along with full-height windows to the front and expansive sliding doors to the back – all triple glazed and slightly tinted for privacy. The way that the house is orientated on the plot means that there is now plenty of light entering from the rear elevation in the mornings and the house is lit from the front in the evenings.

"The home really works well for us. We wanted a home which stood out from the crowd but for a reasonable price and this project definitely delivered. Ultimately though I see the success of the house when people are passing by and they slow down to take a look," says Stuart. "It really is a tribute to Tony and the amazing detail that he put into the design and we now have a scheme which works really well. We were fortunate enough to have a nature reserve at the end of the garden too. It was a case of right plot, right time."

Following the success of this project, has Stuart been bitten by the build bug? "I think it would be a shame not to take everything I've learned and apply it again. I'd absolutely love to do another project and we are already looking!" he admits. "Growing up with parents in the army I was always moving around as a child and even now I only

Thanks to the rear extension, a large open plan kitchen/dining/living space dominates most of the ground floor. The same slate-effect cast concrete tiles used for the exterior have been used to clad the fireplace (see opposite and below) as well as the feature wall in the hallway. Full-height glazed sliding doors break out onto the rear terrace

The kitchen/dining/living area is accessed from the double-height entrance hall; a curved obscured glass wall zones it off

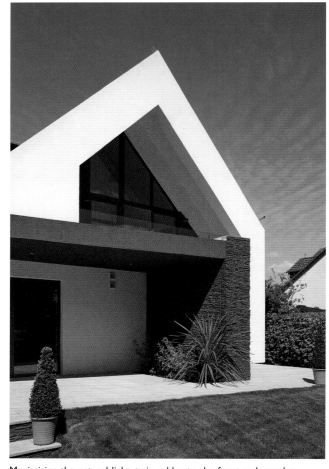

Maximising the natural light, twin gables to the front and rear have been heavily glazed, so the bedrooms upstairs to benefit from full-height views of the surrounding landscape. To the rear, glass doors open out to sheltered balconies with glazed balustrades – providing unobstructed views from two bedrooms

The homeowner's view

With any extension you have to compromise to a point, but we tried to crowbar things in where we could. From the front door you can now see straight through into the garden and the whole space works really well – it's great. Open-plan living brings with it its own set of challenges like noise, but if there are other rooms available for some quiet time then that's not a huge problem. We entertain a lot and so the house works really well for us. It's great to build your "forever home", but think carefully about your projected end-value because it's very easy to go overboard and overdevelop. Ultimately you will want an asset value worth 20-30 percent more than you have spent to justify all your hard work. We wanted a house that stood out from the crowd for a reasonable cost and this home has certainly delivered.

FLOORPLAN

FIRST FLOOR

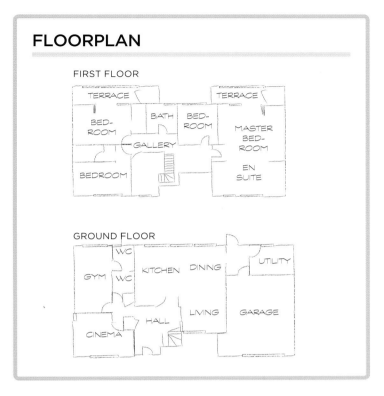

GROUND FLOOR

FACT FILE

Name: Stuart and Elmarie Ward
Area: Dorset
Build type: Contemporary extension and remodel
Size: 380m²

Build date: Sep 2013–Dec 14
Land cost: £310,000
Build cost: £195,000
Cost/m²: £513
House value: £900,000

CONTACTS

Architect Tony Holt (01202 208331; tonyholt-design.co.uk)
Structural engineer Sean Playford (01202 240316)
Bio-ethanol fires, flooring, bathroom sanitaryware, slate-effect cast concrete tiles, external insulation, render,

kitchen and taps Leroy Merlyn, Poland (leroymerlin.com)
Kitchen units TradePoint (trade-point.co.uk)
Builders' merchants Travis Perkins (travisperkins.co.uk) Buildbase (buildbase.co.uk)

Built to Last

A new stone, steel and timber home in Monmouthshire blends traditional materials and forms with modern family living

WORDS: JASON ORME PHOTOGRAPHY: SIMON MAXWELL

The new house, built out of steel frame and clad in a mix of natural stone and timber, draws on the traditional simple barn form. Owners Martin and Kelly bought an old bungalow that had been advertised as "for refurbishment", but decided to replace it – in a different location with better orientation on the valley site

Side Elevation
The stone was cropped and chamfered on one of the window edges and cut with a disc cutter to give it a purposely smooth finish in order to contrast with the more rural finish elsewhere. Note how the window is off centre, but the right-hand side of the window edge is in line with the apex of the roof

Vertical Timber Cladding
Engineered floorboards have been laid vertically in the
double-height dining space, which features a bespoke
glazing panel and large sliding glass door. The steel
structure is very much left on display

Chimney as a Focus
The bulky, solid, stone-clad chimney anchors the house
externally, but it is a feature to be enjoyed from the inside
too. An outside fireplace makes the transition between
inside and out even more seamless

The landing is supported by long steel beams and enjoys views over the double-height dining space. Martin and Kelly decided to leave the steel beams exposed to give the home an even greater sense of solidity and honesty about its barn-style structure

The architect/owner project (an architect designing a project for themselves) is usually a recipe for disaster – a chance for the frustrated designer, finally unfettered after all those years of having to compromise on pent-up ideas due to clients who rather inconveniently want what they want, is free to unleash all sorts of bonkers features and 'clever' concepts on a one-off house. With nobody to say no to them, the house ends up a statement calling card and all too often a total write-off.

Well – Martin Hall and Kelly Bednarczyk's house is the exact opposite of all that. It is, without fear of exaggeration, a truly exceptional testament to how high-quality, thoughtful design can meet well-considered, sensitive specification and result in a truly family-orientated home that is both of a human scale – the house is 240m² – and yet truly awe-inspiring.

The happy compromises that Martin and Kelly, who run the award-winning Chepstow architectural firm that takes their surnames (and who won a Daily Telegraph Homebuilding & Renovating Award a couple of years ago), contended with were the fact that this had to work as a family home and at the same time, as Martin admits: "We didn't have a massive budget. This had to make sense for us." If there is one lesson you should take away from this house it is that high-quality design features needn't be an additional cost. Good spaces can be good value and the house is full of 'ordinary' materials being used in extraordinary ways.

"We were looking to move," begins Martin, "and discovered agent's details for a Sixties bungalow on a rocky, one-acre site. What we loved about it was that despite being at the bottom of the valley it got plenty of sun and the views were fantastic. The bungalow was really sold as a doer-upper but we took it on realising it could be totally transformed."

And totally transform the plot they did. Keeping the existing house as a temporary home, Martin and Kelly managed to convince the planners to let them build a new house and reorientate it through 90° so that not only did it enjoy the views but the new rectangular form could be on an east-west axis. Martin's theory is that while everyone is really obsessed by building houses north-

Family Bathroom
Vertically biased fixed glazing from Velfac provides natural light without affecting privacy. The tiles are from Porcelanosa, with sanitaryware from Duravit and taps from Crosswater

Wardrobes were built in to the walls in the master bedroom. Because of the volumetric height of the space, the wardrobes help to give the external walls a greater sense of thickness and solidity. Blinds are recessed into the walls

south, building them across the east/west axis allows bedrooms to be positioned to enjoy the morning sun.

What came next was a feeling of what Martin calls: "Being drawn to the no-nonsense solidity of the barn conversion." The simple grid pattern of the building made it relatively straightforward to design, built around a steel frame structure with, in effect, a chequer pattern series of blanks and solids (windows and cladding). Indeed the steel frame is one of the house's unsung victories, and Martin and Kelly have added some galvanized steel channel sections to express the structural steel frame that lies directly beneath, as otherwise it would have been completely hidden in the insulated build-up.

One of the great magical touches about this house is its scale – it's almost a trick of the eye in many ways. Because of its positioning surrounded by woodland and because of its window positions and 'domestic' feel it looks, from a distance (and in a photographic shoot) actually quite small. Yet up close it's in fact quite imposing and impressive – the flat frontage (save for a beautiful chunky chimney) and large glazing gives a real sense of 'wow.' Indeed the chimney is perhaps Martin and Kelly's favourite part of the house – it anchors the building to the ground and even incorporates an outdoor fireplace.

"Actually, this house was all about maximising architectural wow for the money," says Kelly (the budget was £350,000, coming out at £1,450/m²). Inside, the one-room deep floorplan (it makes it sound small but the depth is 7m or so) allows plenty of light to penetrate – there simply aren't any dark areas. The plan is simple. To the left, as you enter, is the family kitchen and dining space (with a utility and boot space); to the right, after the downstairs loo and plentiful built-in storage, a fantastic living space. Upstairs, a couple of children's bedrooms and a void overlooking the dining table – that 'wow' that Kelly talked about is definitely achieved here – and a fantastic vaulted master bedroom suite that, thanks to the one-room deep layout,

enjoys a triple aspect. It's simple, smart and hugely attractive. With 2.9m ceiling heights throughout, the relatively modest footprint works very hard to give a sense of space.

Kelly calls it: "A robust family home." There is plenty of storage to deal with the rigours of having two young children around and is built with Martin and Kelly's family at the forefront. Yet, because Martin and Kelly are such talented designers, they have managed to incorporate all of these details and features which, almost without thinking about it, improve

Kitchen

Martin and Kelly managed to bring in the whole kitchen – including everything from worktops and appliances to units and taps – for under £12,000. A series of 300mm IKEA end units line up to form the cabinetry. The granite worktop (from Bristol Marble and Granite) on the large and very impressive 1600mm island has a leathered finish to give it a softer, matt feel

livability – all on a scale that isn't beyond many people setting out to build their own home. Above all, the home is a statement for the power of good design.

FLOORPLAN

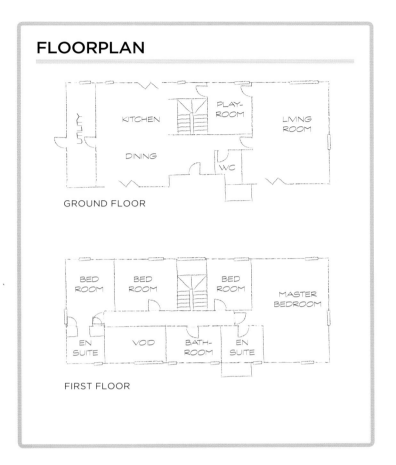

GROUND FLOOR

FIRST FLOOR

FACT FILE

Name: Martin Hall and Kelly Bednarczyk
Area: Monmouthshire
Build type: Barn-style self-build
Size: 240m2

Build date: Sep 2012- Aug 13
Land cost: £296,000
Build cost: £350,000
Cost/m²: £1,458
House value: £750,000

CONTACTS

Architect Hall + Bednarczyk Architects (01291 627777 hallbednarczyk.com)
Main contractor MacCormac Construction (01873 851712)
Structural engineer Azimuth Structural Engineering (01452 561000)
Energy consultant Paul Thornton Design (01594 832300)
Ecology consultant Abbey Sanders Ecology (07962 172453)
Heating and plumbing Alan Reynolds Heating (01873 857483)
Oak sliding windows and stairs Advance Joinery (01981 241071)

Windows Velfac (01223 897100)
Steel frame Remnant Engineering (01594 841160)
Kitchen island and worktops Bristol Marble & Granite (0117 965 6565)
Kitchen sinks and taps Franke (0161 436 6280)
Kitchen appliances Smeg (0844 557 9907)
Kitchen units IKEA (020 3645 0000)
Sanitaryware Duravit (0845 500 7787)
Bathroom taps and showers Crosswater (0845 873 8840)
Bathroom tiles Bathroom Solutions (Bristol) (01225 335664)

The homeowners' view

With this house we aimed to create a family home that has a very strong affinity with its rural setting. The design used simple, confident massing combined with a contemporary use of regional materials – the stone was quarried three miles away. The relative privacy of the house's rural location enabled generous glazing to be employed that illuminates the living spaces with natural light as well as framing views of the surrounding landscape, which feels like it passes through the home.

The floorplan (right) is based on a simple barn design prioritising larger rather than more rooms. On the ground floor, the large kitchen/dining space and living room bookend the layout – linked by a playroom that can be closed off or opened up as required. Storage – essential with a young family – is everywhere. Upstairs, we decided to sacrifice a bedroom for the void over the double-height dining space below. Even so, there are four generous- sized bedrooms.

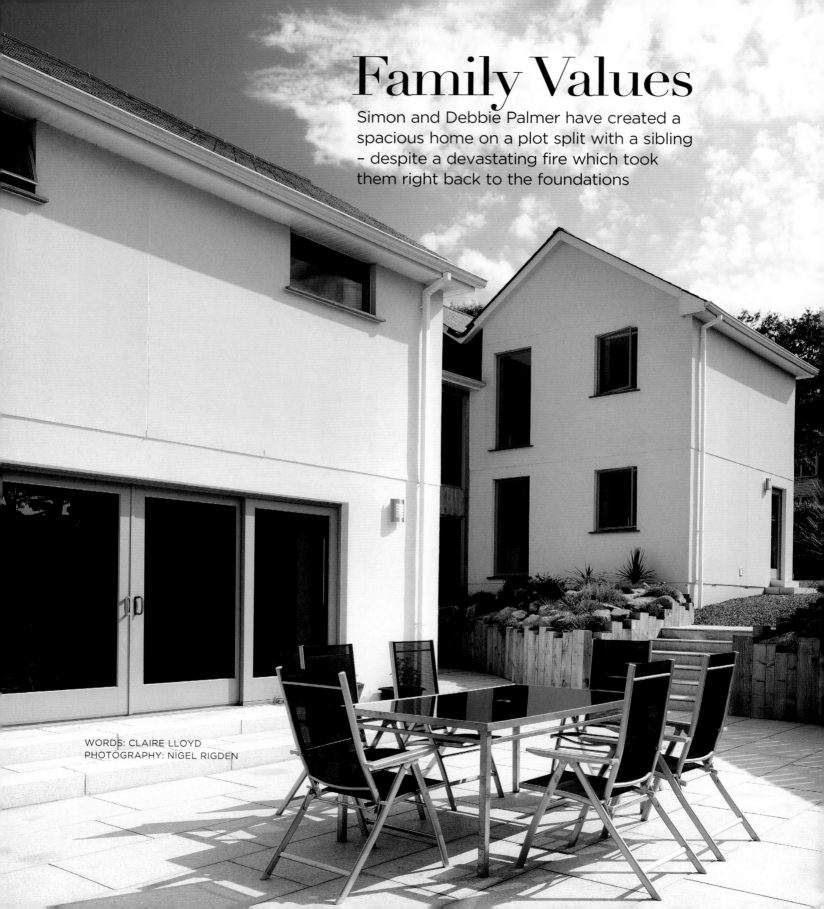

Family Values

Simon and Debbie Palmer have created a spacious home on a plot split with a sibling – despite a devastating fire which took them right back to the foundations

WORDS: CLAIRE LLOYD
PHOTOGRAPHY: NIGEL RIGDEN

The house features a number of curves – from the sculptural staircase to the timber-clad barrel-shaped addition at the rear (which houses a spacious dining space with galleried landing)

If a predisposition to self-build could be passed down through the generations, then Simon Palmer has surely inherited the gene. Not only has he followed in his parent's footsteps by taking a hands-on role in building his own property, but the very site on which it sits was once home to his grandparent's self-built bungalow. Despite this pedigree, Simon and wife Debbie's route to creating a home to share with sons Callum and Sam was not all plain sailing – thanks to a fire which would take them from a weathertight shell right back to the foundations.

The result of the determined couple's endeavour is however a family home of contemporary styling, featuring white render and cedar cladding to the angular, street-facing façade. Despite the straight lines here, small 'portholes' punctuating the front door are not simply testament to the house's coastal location – which is within a short commute of Plymouth – but hint at the sweeping curves which lie behind, within the crisp, white interiors. Such curves begin with the sculptural staircase which welcomes guests (more on this later), and conclude quite spectacularly in the double-height dining space, contained within a barrel-like addition, to the rear.

The couple's ideas for their new home first began to take shape in 2007 when the decision was taken to divide the inherited Seventies bungalow and spacious, sloping garden into two plots: one for the couple and the other for Simon's sister, Lisa, and brother-in-law,

Differing ceiling heights providw
visual definition between the dining
room and kitchen

The kitchen/breakfast room features white gloss
kitchen cupboards which bounce light around the
room; a bold splashback injects colour

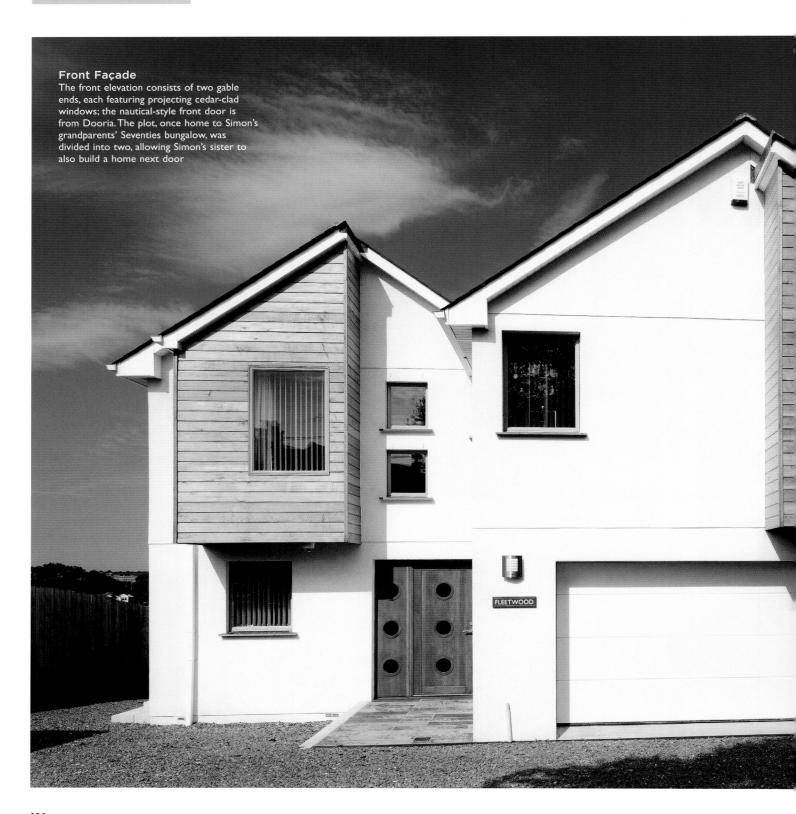

Front Façade

The front elevation consists of two gable ends, each featuring projecting cedar-clad windows; the nautical-style front door is from Dooria. The plot, once home to Simon's grandparents' Seventies bungalow, was divided into two, allowing Simon's sister to also build a home next door

FLEETWOOD

Mike. "We knew if we built the two properties together we could get much better deals on purchasing materials," explains Simon. And so, local architect Chris Jones was engaged at the close of 2007 to design two complimentary modern homes.

Obtaining planning permission proved relatively straightforward, allowing work to begin on site in June 2008. "The first thing dad advised was buying a second-hand mini-digger," says Simon, who took on the project management role alongside his father, Nick. The bungalow was duly demolished and grubbed up, clearing the way for the groundworkers to prepare the foundations. The existing garage was, however, maintained to provide a site office and useful storage space. Plumbing in a toilet here too saved on the cost of hiring one in.

With his father on hand to manage proceedings during the day, Simon was on site every evening after work, before returning to the couple's Plymouth-based flat. "Working full time and trying to do the build with a very young family was extremely hard on everyone," he says.

By April 2009, the family's hard work had paid off as less than 12 months after breaking ground, both houses were weathertight, ready for the local trades to begin first fix inside. "But on May 6th I was woken at 3.30am by a call from my brother-in-law telling us that our two houses were on fire! I jumped in the car and drove 15 miles to be met by several fire engines and police," Simon explains regretfully. "They'd managed to save my sister's house with only minor damage to

Savvy savings

At 302m², the Palmers have achieved a spacious home for their build budget of £225,000; this is due in no small part to their savvy material specification, with many purchases made in bulk in order to negotiate a discount. "We ordered all the bathroom tiles from one company for example," explains Simon of the Porcelanosa tiles which have been installed in the main bathroom and two en suites. Shopping around also aided.

Project managing and taking on tasks on a DIY basis was invariably key to keeping a handle on costs too. "It's things such as specifying door sets which meant there was minimal labour involved that helped to cut down costs too," says Simon of the Dooria door sets which come complete with hinges and locks fitted.

In addition to the mini-digger, the Palmers decided to invest in tools which would again allow them to take on further tasks on a DIY basis. "We bought quite a few tools to help, like a Paslode nail gun and cordless autofeed screwdriver for the plasterboarding," says Simon. "When we finished, we sold them on eBay for only a little less than we bought them for."

the roof slates, solar panels and render. Seeing our new home smouldering away was heartbreaking to say the least."

Fortunately the £1,500 which the couple had invested in insurance proved its weight in gold, with their BuildStore inspector visiting the site two days later. Both the inspector and fire brigade's report concluded that the fire had been started by arson. "We were left feeling really hurt that someone could do that to our dream home," Simon adds.

Insurance funds were duly released and the couple, with the help of family and friends, picked themselves up to begin the process again. "Because of the contamination from the fire we had to go back to the footings and rebuild virtually from scratch.

"It did however give us the opportunity to slightly alter the design," says Simon. "We'd originally built a three storey glazed turret-like structure to the front elevation, which was going to serve as an office, but we decided to do away with this second time around."

Timber frame was again used for a fast construction. Timber came again to the forefront in the house's pièce de résistance: the sculptural staircase. "At the time of building the house, we couldn't find anyone manufacturing curved staircases in timber in the UK," says Simon. Eventually, thorough internet research led them to a Polish company. "We contacted their Cornish agent and went to visit another property which featured an example of their work," says Simon. "The main staircase was definitely our best purchase! We love it and it gets the most comments by visitors at how spectacular it looks."

Their home will also provide them with low running costs thanks to the photovoltaic panels, and a 5,000litre rainwater harvesting system, which now provides water for the washing machine, all four toilets as well as an ample supply for watering the landscaped garden.

"After everything that happened we have come out the other side stronger, happier and have a better house than we ever envisaged," reflects Simon. "The children love it and so do we."

Breakfast Bar
A kitchen/breakfast room, providing an informal spot to sit with a coffee, overlooks the dramatic dining area, which is partially open to a galleried landing above

FLOORPLAN

GROUND FLOOR

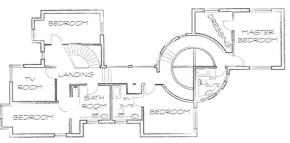

FIRST FLOOR

Practical rooms such as the garage, utility and downstairs WC have been positioned to the front of the house, allowing the rest of the ground floor to be given over to a kitchen/breakfast room, with an open plan dining space and living area set below. On the first floor, the boys have their own rooms and share a family bathroom and TV/games room. To the rear, the master en suite – which features a large dressing room – is separated by a galleried landing. There's also an en suite guest room.

FACT FILE

Name: Simon and Debbie Palmer
Area: Cornwall
Build type: Self-build
Size: 305m²

Build date: July 2008–Oct 10
Land cost: £150,000
Build cost: £225,000
Cost/m²: £750
House value: Unknown

CONTACTS

Architect Chris Jones (01208 873234)
Groundworks Phil Punter (07976 819774)
Timber frame Frame 2000 (01446 742287)
Blockwork and roofing KJ Channings (07789 764452)
Andersen windows and patio doors, Dooria front and internal doors, and skirting Door Stop (Truro) (01872 261260)
Tiles Porcelanosa Western (Exeter) (01395 215552)
Landscaping and gardens A & J Builders (07968 963332)
Cedar cladding, wood flooring and fencing Bond Timber (Cornwall) (01503 240308)
Stairs and balustrades Janusz

@ Polishproducts (00485 01511601)
Kitchen and utility room Bradburys (Exeter) (01392 825940)
Bathrooms Ivybridge Tile and Bathroom (01752 897800)
Electric gates Westcountry Gates and Barriers (01752 338990)
Electrics PC Doney Electrics (07768 377012)
Carpets Premier Carpets (Launceston) (01566 775010)
Underfloor heating Nu-Heat (0800 731 1976)
Whole house ventilation system Villavent (01993 778481)
Bespoke oak dining table and furniture Oakwerke (07875 799391)

"Purchase as many materials as you can yourself and shop around – there are lots of discounts available and all the builders' merchants are fighting for your business. Don't just presume that the price you received last time is still the best as deals change regularly"

Simple Living

Following the demolition of a post-war bungalow on a family plot, Louise and Ivor Nicholson have successfully built a contemporary new eco home on a tight budget

WORDS: CAROLINE EDNIE   PHOTOGRAPHY: NIGEL RIGDEN

The large open plan kitchen/dining/living space is the hub of family life. The sleek Howdens kitchen overlooks the family area which is cleverly zoned, thanks to the large (3.5m) BoConcept corner sofa

I t's quite a stretch of the imagination to believe that Louise and Ivor Nicholson's striking new family home in rural Aberdeenshire actually started life as a plan to extend a modest 65m² post-war bungalow which had been in Louise's family for the last quarter of a century – a stretch too given that the proposed extension had already been through the early stages of the planning process.

There were, however, a couple of defining moments which quickly changed the couple's mind: principally the quantity surveyor's assessment, which (taking into account the inevitable VAT that would have to be paid) meant that the final cost was verging on "scary". This brought home the realisation that it would cheaper to demolish and remove the house than to amend it.

"To do the stripping out of the original house was going to cost £12,000, whereas demolishing it and removing it from site (which in the end only took two days) was only likely to cost £9,000. It was a

no-brainer," explains the Nicholson's architect, David Wilson of Aberdeen-based Room Architects.

Luckily, Louise wasn't too sentimental about the thought of replacing her former family home, which was lying empty at the time of the couple's decision to take it on. "It was very cramped and damp, but my family would never have sold it on as the garden and the surrounding views all the way down to the Balmedie sand dunes are fantastic," says Louise, who was the main driving force of the project, and managed a large part of sourcing the items for the internal finishes of the completed house.

With the decision made to demolish and rebuild, graphic designer Louise had very clear ideas about the design of the family's new home and went back to the drawing board with architect David Wilson. "We were living at the time in a flat in a Victorian granite building in Aberdeen city, which we loved, but starting from scratch, we knew

Light-Filled Interiors
Full-height Velfac windows and a feature
window from Olsen allow natural daylight
to flood through the open-plan family space

The interior colour scheme is predominantly white, with light oak flooring from Blueridge Flooring – taking a cue from Scandinavian-style design

that we wanted a modern house," explains Louise. "My taste tends towards Scandinavian design, so what I had in mind was a simple white and glass box with a flat roof."

Trying to convince the local planning authority of their plans for a pared-down, minimalist construction amidst Aberdeenshire's flat farmland wasn't going to be easy though. "There were serious structural issues with the existing house," says architect David Wilson, "and from an environmental point of view, it couldn't be seen as an effective and energy-efficient long-term family home, so we managed to prove to the planners that the existing house wasn't a viable option. But, in terms of the new design, the planners were keen to retain the main elements of the existing house, which was a slate pitch roof over white rendered walls, which we've echoed in the form and colour of the new house."

What emerged following a 10-month construction period is a contemporary new 155m² single storey family home, built using a bespoke timber kit with Kingspan insulation packed both between and outside of the frame, and complete with a smooth, low-maintenance rendered blockwork exterior. The roof was originally intended to be zinc, but was later substituted for Colorcoat Urban® Tata seam steel in an effort to save on costs.

In order to meet the planner's requirements for a more effective, energy-efficient home, and the couple's desire to introduce renewable solutions (see right), the home has been designed to harness energy from the sun, as well as bring in light to the interior spaces. "The house is orientated so that it follows the sun's path through the day," explains David of his design solution. "The idea was to align the windows in order to harness light at certain times of the day. So, for

Sitting within Aberdeenshire's rural landscape, the home benefits from far-reaching views towards Balmedie's sand dunes. A large picture window with sliding door has been introduced into the living space in order to capture the views of the surrounding landscape – it opens out onto a decked area and garden beyond

"Don't scrimp on the most important details of the design. We spent a lot on the insulation, and the house performs so well in this regard as a result. The glazing was also expensive but it's really fantastic that we can use many openings as doors as well as windows"

example, the bedroom windows get the morning sun to wake you up." Photovoltaic panels were then installed to the garage roof to capture the sun, the savings of which help to offset the cost of the electricity required to run the ground-source heat pump installed in the garden; the latter powers the underfloor heating.

In terms of the interiors, the home has effectively been divided into two. One half is dedicated to an open plan living/kitchen/dining space, with light flooding in from three directions thanks in part to large lift-and-slide Velfac windows which open out to the south-east elevation, and offer great views towards the beach. The living room area is also a particular highlight with its double-height space up into the apex of the roof which features clean lines and no structural ties. The second half of the home has been designed as a dedicated bedroom wing with four bedrooms – one with an en suite – a family bathroom and storage space. A separate utility room also helps to hide clutter.

The internal fittings were very much a family effort, with Ivor, an electrician by trade (who also fortunately had a trade account) taking care of the electrical work, with other family members (all, fortuitously enough, skilled tradesmen) taking care of other aspects of the build, including the engineered oak timber flooring, the kitchen and bathroom fit-outs. Calling on family favours also meant that costs could be kept within the impressive (and tight) £185,000 budget.

"We were always trying to claw money back, but we were keen to keep important design features, such as the clean lines of the guttering and details like the shadow gaps in the skirtings," explains Louise of the project, which the couple funded by selling a city flat they owned, and finally through the sale of their own Aberdeen flat, which they stayed in during the construction of their new home.

"We did have to make some compromises. But then I think that what I've got within our budget is amazing!" concludes Louise.

FACT FILE

Name: Louise and Ivor Nicholson
Area: Aberdeenshire
Build type: Self-build
Size: 155m²

Build time: 10 months
Land cost: £0 (already owned)
Build cost: £185,882
Cost/m²: £1,160
House value: unknown

CONTACTS

Architect Room Architects (01330 830088)
Structural engineer McKenzie Willis (01224 639111)
Quantity surveyor Beedie Mitchell (01224 623166)
Main contractor, construction frame and roofing Chapman Homes (01467 621397)
K Rend render finish Muirfield (01382 810000)
Plumbing and heating East Coast Eco Systems

(0800 690 6977)
Windows Velfac (01223 897100)
Olsen (01777 874510)
Sanitaryware Duravit (duravit.co.uk)
Kitchen and appliances Howdens (howdens.com)
Insulation Kingspan (kingspan.com)
Flooring Blueridge Flooring (0330 123 9262)

FLOORPLAN

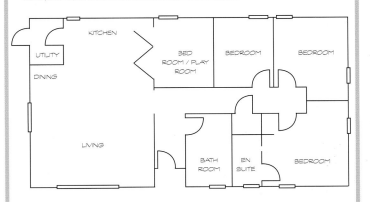

Mew Stone East makes the most of its estuary views by placing the living accommodation on the top floor, which boasts an open plan kitchen diner stepping down to a large living area and terrace. The middle floor houses an en suite guest bedroom with courtyard, and the master suite, complete with dressing area, en suite and terrace. The lower floor (not shown) includes three bedrooms (two en suite), a family bathroom and laundry.

A labour of love

Richard and Chrissie Baker's timber frame self-built home on the Isle of Man is a triumph of determination and inspiration

WORDS: JASON ORME   PHOTOGRAPHY: JEREMY PHILLIPS

The new home successfully navigates the challenges of a sloping site, with a formwork basement holding cantilevered steels which support the overhanging deck and Potton timber frame. The cedar cladding was all fitted by Richard

A LABOUR OF LOVE

If you happened to wander past Richard and Chrissie Baker's then-building site some three and a half years ago you would have found Richard partway through shifting 220 tonnes – 220 tonnes! – of rubble, dug out to make way for their basement walls, back into position around now-built walls. By wheelbarrow. Each barrow fed by a digger that Richard had spent £5,000 or so on when they started. Richard remembers that he wheeled 50 barrowloads a day, every day for five months. You just hope he had a good wheelbarrow.

Richard and Chrissie were determined to tackle almost all of the building work themselves. The huge amount of DIY involvement clearly enabled them to feel much more connected to the finished home and it is an absolute triumph of hard work, determination and that spirit of "can-do" entrepeneurship that typifies the best self-builds – this one included.

With the exception of some of the groundworks, the basement formwork, some steelwork and all of the timber-frame, he and Chrissie went on to effectively build the home single-handed over a period of four years, two of which he fitted in around his work, two of which were full-time upon his retirement. To call this self-build barely does it justice.

"We've had a lifetime of doing up homes," explains Chrissie in the sun-drenched kitchen of their now complete home, which enjoys glimpses of the sea in a lovely hidden corner of the north-east of the Isle of Man. "We moved eight times in 20 years and I built up some considerable experience of working around the house," says Richard. "We always wanted to do one from scratch. All the other homes, regardless of what we achieved, had some degree of compromise. We wanted to build our own home to truly get what we wanted."

Plots on the Isle are sparse and when an opportunity came up, Richard and Chrissie had to move fast. "It was around a third of an acre, heavily wooded and sloping – it was effectively the bottom of the garden of a house up the hill," explains Chrissie. "We could see it would have great views, and decided to go for it." Given the location to local areas of historical interest, their offer was made subject to the satisfactory outcome of a geophysical survey, assessing the site too for any archeological interest which would have put the kibosh on any development. When this was received, the couple went ahead and acquired the plot, which came with outline planning permission.

That's when Richard and Chrissie really got going. "We wanted to build a home to our very own design and specification without compromise. We wanted a contemporary but un-fussy design with lots of glass, inside/outside living, open plan living area and a garage underneath. The house had to be low energy with the plumbing all located in the same quarter of the house to reduce pipe runs.

"On this project we didn't use an architect, a Quantity Surveyor or a project manager," says Richard. Instead Chrissie and Richard

A woodburning stove, from Stoves Online, is only really used for effect, thanks to the house's excellent energy efficiency and MVHR unit. The large circular features are acoustic baffles, countering any sonic problems from the high ceiling (2.9m), the glass and the hard floors

spent endless hours planning and designing their dream home on a fairly simple piece of home design software, using magazines and the internet to guide their schemes. "That was one of the many benefits for us of using Potton, the timber frame supplier," says Richard. "Their service stretched well beyond simply designing and erecting the kit. They turned all our conceptual drawings into real working constructional drawings, as well as drawings to submit for planning. They helped with everything and kept in touch throughout the project – the service was excellent." The contemporary scheme, which Richard had informally ran past a planning officer before submitting, was approved without trouble.

"We knew we wanted our home to be as energy efficient as possible," says Richard. But, given the island setting, local expertise on cutting-edge PassivHaus-style site practice was lacking – leaving Richard to take the lead in minimising energy use. "We considered SIPs but in the end went for Potton's closed panel timber frame system, maxing out the Kingspan insulation to 120mm (achieving U-values of 0.15(?) in the process.) The basement is built out of concrete formwork, with steel beams cantilevering out to provide support for the deck. The timber frame sits off the basement walls. Triple-glazed windows from Internorm provide excellent performance throughout (U-values around 0.8 compared to typical double glazing of 1.6) as well as pleasing looks – large areas of glazing with minimal frames and lovely large sliding doors. The heating system consists of an Earthsave 4kW heat pump powering underfloor heating with an MVHR (mechanical ventilation with heat recovery) system from

The large kitchen flows into the dining and living space (note the lack of internal doors). Amtico vinyl flooring provides the perfect surface over underfloor heating

Energy Efficiency

Minimising long-term running costs was very important to Richard and Chrissie, so in addition to the high-spec wall build-ups (120mm of Kingspan in the timber frame) they have also added solar PV panels, placed behind parapets on the flat roof to hide them. The large windows in the kitchen are triple-glazed. Richard did almost all of his own plumbing and heating engineering, and the plant room is immaculately organised, housing everything from the buffer tanks to the underfloor-heating manifold

Genvex managing ventilation as well as using heat generated in the kitchen and bathrooms to help heat the rest of the home. With a woodburner providing bags of heat for the open plan ground floor space, Richard and Chrissie have had the underfloor heating on a grand total of once over the 15 months they have lived in the house. In many ways the key issue is controlling overheating, which they have accounted for in the design (covered outdoor spaces minimising direct sunlight) and specification (the Internorm windows are coated to reduce solar gain – the triple glazing helps in this regard too). Fifteen PV panels hidden behind a parapet on the flat roof (single ply membrane) provide a significant contribution to the bills. LED lights throughout minimise energy use.

Sound performance was important to Richard and Chrissie too – having noticed the occasionally echo-ey nature of some modern builds with lots of glass, hard floors and high ceilings. "After completion we found a firm (Sonata Acoustics) who specialised in commercial buildings who would provide acoustic panels," says Chrissie. "They sit on the ceiling and some walls and make a massive difference. In a way they have become a bit of a feature in their own right," she says.

As an example of the evolution of timber frame packages, Richard and Chrissie's home is outstanding – on several levels. Not least that it marks the evolution of design in this sector – it is difficult to imagine one our longest-established timber frame companies building something like this a decade ago – but also that it stands as an example of the performance and desirability of timber-frame homes in their own right.

When most of us think of timber frame homes, we think of traditional styles, conservative layouts and, frankly, function over form. It might conjure up the idea of 'out of the brochure' designs from a handful of house styles. What the Bakers' home exemplifies is that timber frame is a perfectly sensible option for those looking to build beautiful bespoke homes at the top end of contemporary architecture: that, most importantly, using a timber frame company now means you're open to exciting design in the same way that you would be using an independent architect. Richard and Chrissie Baker's home pushes forward the image of timber-frame homes – and shows what can be achieved.

The scale of Richard and Chrissie's endeavours takes some comprehending. To list but a few of their achievements, between them they handled the blockwork, all of the plumbing and electrics, drainage, bathroom and kitchen fitting, installation of the Western Red Cedar timber cladding and much else besides the finishes and all the landscaping. Just imagine having to install 300 sheets of Fermacel boards (at 40kg each). And that's only a fraction of the job. "The truth is that a lot of the work on a build site requires only modest skill levels," claims Richard, modestly. You can learn an awful lot simply by reading installation manuals and, of course, researching on the internet. It took its time to build, but we're delighted with it."

FLOORPLAN

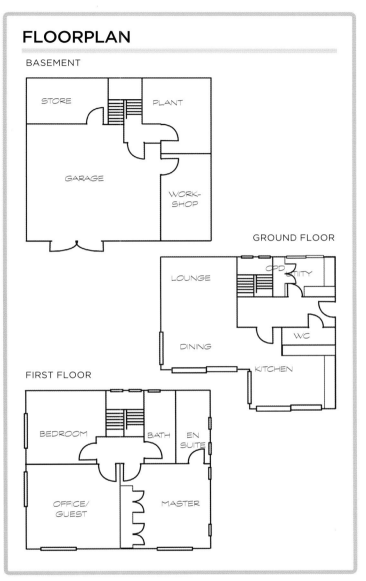

BASEMENT

STORE

PLANT

GARAGE

WORK-SHOP

GROUND FLOOR

LOUNGE

CPD

UTILITY

DINING

WC

KITCHEN

FIRST FLOOR

BEDROOM

BATH

EN SUITE

OFFICE/GUEST

MASTER

FACT FILE

Name: Richard and Chrissie Baker
Area: Isle of Man
Build type: Timber-frame self-build
Size: 285m²

Build date: Oct 2010–July 14
Land cost: £270,000
Build cost: £398,000
Total cost: £668,000
House value: £675,000
Cost/m²: £1,396

CONTACTS

Timber frame Potton (01767 676400)
Windows Internorm (020 8205 9991)
Flooring Amtico (01212 228 757)
Blinds Luxaflex (luxaflex.co.uk)
MVHR Total Home Environment (0345 260 0123)
Heat Pump Earthsave Products (01865 598 158)
Bathroom Panels Altro (01462 489 516)
Appliances Appliances Direct (0871 984 4416)
Plasterboard Fermacel (0121 311 3480)
Western Red Cedar Cladding Silva Timber (0151 541 8562)
Sanitaryware Laufen (01530 510007)
Garage Door Hormann (01530 513000)
General Building Materials Island Timber & Building Materials (01624 827336)
J. Qualtrough & Co (01624 822581)
Macs Builders Merchants (01624 844588)
Jewson (01624 813389)
C. Kniveton (01624 828840)
CuPlas Callow Ltd (01624 618169)
Corlett Building Materials

(01624 842200)
Bathrooms Riverside Ceramics Ltd (01624 619539)
Electrical products QVS (01483 569559)
Plumbing, electrical and fastenings Toolstation (0808 1007211)
External Balustrade Balcony Systems Solutions (01342 410411)
Internal door sets Silvelox (0800 9151019)
Electric gate components The Electric Gate Shop (01405 785656)
Composite Decking Timco Wood UK Ltd. (01707 331200)
Electrical TLC (01293 565630)
Woodburning Stove & Flue Stovesonline (0845 2265754)
Solion Sunmouts for solar panels UFW (0116 2581410)
Solar Panels Navitron (01572 725512)
LED Downlights Expert Electrical Supplies (01706 860011)
Underfloor Heating UFH Trade Direct (01925 571999)
Acoustic Panels Sonata Acoustics Ltd (01977 799252)
Garage Floor Tiles Stormflame (01329 841416)

"On this project we didn't use an architect, a Quantity Surveyor or a project manager"

Fred and Edna's new home replaces a derelict bungalow. The site is heavily sloping to the front – some 6m higher to the rear – and the main living accommodation is on the ground floor. The lower ground floor, which has been partially built into the site, is home to the bedrooms and utility spaces

On Reflection

Edna Wadham's son, architect Paul Archer, has created a remarkable new home on a sloping site for her and husband Fred

WORDS: JASON ORME PHOTOGRAPHY: SIMON MAXWELL

It seems that Fred and Edna Wadham don't like to take the easy route. Spotting a dilapidated bungalow on a half-acre River Severn estuary site – which had such a slope down to the road that it is 6m higher at the top of the plot than the bottom – they have not only replaced it with a contemporary scheme that features remarkably futuristic cladding, but the house has an unconventional (but kind of back-to-nature) heating system and, to cap it all, required a sort of mastery of the site that most ordinary people would have tried to avoid. Oh, and Fred even ended up handling most of the fittings and finishings himself after running into bother with the builders.

Luckily, the couple did have one important asset in their corner: Edna's son, Paul Archer, is an award-winning architect (Paul Archer Design) and could help come up with a concept that not only solved the issues that the plot presented, but also created what is a highly impressive piece of house design that has presented Fred and Edna with a home that is everything their previous house wasn't – light, flowing and efficient.

"We loved the position of the site and knew we wanted to build something that our previous homes weren't," begins Edna. "Paul's design was brilliant in its own right but perfect for the site. Our brief was for a Californian-style house with green credentials – one that would permit seamless indoor/outdoor living while delivering a zero-carbon agenda. Essentially, we wanted a modern, light and airy house, which takes advantage of the views."

The resulting scheme consists of an excavated blockwork construction for the lower ground floor, which is sunken into the site, with a lightweight timber frame 'ground' floor on top. The latter is used for the main open plan living space and master bedroom (the nature of the site allows direct access from this level to the garden, although the main entrance is via the lower ground floor). The upstairs open plan space is a real triumph – there's woodburning stoves to provide spot heating, but the whole home is centrally heated by a wood-fired Esse range (the only heat source in the house – see right). Two external terraces connect to the garden and are orientated to catch the sun at different times of the day.

The eco credentials of the house are hugely impressive, from design to specification – making it one of the most self-sufficient houses we've seen. Water, for instance, is supplied by a 93m-deep borehole, while thermal solar panels yield heating for 80 per cent of the home's hot water and photovoltaic panels provide all of the electricity when taken over a year's cycle. There's also a sedum roof which helps to regulate the internal temperature.

It is, of course, the motorised aluminium panels that are the main talking point of the house though. "They created quite a stir with the planning application," recalls Edna. "Even now I'm not

The open plan ground floor features a kitchen, living and dining area. An Esse wood-fired range cooker provides hot water for whole-house heating, as well as cooking. The white IKEA units have been paired with white corian worktops

The house features a lightweight ground floor timber frame sat on blockwork at lower ground floor level (which is partially built into the sloping site). The ground floor has been finished in sliding motorised timber panels that are clad in reflective aluminium, which reflect the surrounding trees. The panels close over the windows, providing security and privacy

One benefit of having the bedrooms on the lower ground floor is that they are connected to the outdoor spaces. And, thanks to the sloping nature of the site, parts of the upper storey connect too. The lower ground floor is built in blockwork; the ground floor is constructed from a lightweight timber frame

The Stûv woodburning stove provides useful additional spot heating in the open plan living space. The low-maintenance polished concrete floor is from Shortman

sure all of the neighbours are fully on side!" The panels are in fact bespoke, hand-crafted timber boards that are clad with mirrored aluminium. Fully motorised and controllable, Fred and Edna can use them to shut the house off or open it up on demand – the panels have a significant impact on the thermal performance of the house itself too, as well as being an impressive security measure. Despite their undoubted futuristic appeal, the panels also help to bed the house into its environment in that they (obviously) reflect the trees and garden, rather than stand out in the way that, say, a white rendered finish might.

Indeed, the landscape is one of the home's crowning achievements. A sunken driveway and raised garden reduces the visual impact of the new home and provides a perfect setting for this most interesting of schemes. The current tranquility of the site hides a rather tumultuous building experience, however, with the main contractors going bust with the shell of the house up, covered in blue lining, and a long way from being finished. This meant that the couple ended up having to camp out for a year in the house while Fred polished off his rather impressive carpentry skills to finish the house, including fitting those aluminium panels to the exterior and the stunning interior glass balustrading.

"From the nature of the site to the innovative nature of the design, and problems with the project, it has been far from straightforward," says Edna. "But we've ended up with a wonderful house that is a pleasure to live in, that's very efficient and cheap to run, and in a great spot. It was definitely worth pushing the boat out for."

Range cookers

The house's traditional wood-fired, cast iron range cooker supplies hot water for the central heating system as well as performing as a standard cooker. The appeal of woodburning ranges is obvious: no energy bills and the ability to produce a clean and reliable form of whole-house heating.

They are not without their problems. When it burns, it really burns, and produces lots of unused heat that needs dumping. And they require maintenance – clearing out the ash can be quite repetitive. "We only need to remove the ash once a month," says Fred. That is thanks to a combination of two things – the stove's high combustion performance (it burns up more of the material) and high-quality wood, which again means that more can be burned for heat rather than left behind. The house's Esse model has a range of controls (oven bypass, different door opening settings) that enable a fire to be drawn up quickly and then eased down: much more control than you might expect.

These particular Esse models also connect into a thermostatically controlled boiler with the option of summer performance, allowing the range cooker to heat up sufficiently to provide domestic hot water, without needing to supply the radiators or underfloor heating. "We love it," says Fred. "It's easy to control and we enjoy the interaction with it. It's obviously very cheap to run. But much more than that, you feel very connected to nature."

FACT FILE

Name: Fred and Edna Wadham
Area: Gloucestershire
Build type: Self-build
Size: 200m²
Build date: Nov 2008–Sept 11

Land cost: £212,000
Build cost: £500,000
Cost/m²: £2,500
House value: Unknown

CONTACTS

Design Paul Archer Design
(020 3668 2668)
Structural engineer Fluid
Structures (020 7820 7766)
M&E engineer Clearsprings
Energy Solutions
(03300 881451)
Quantity surveyor Dickson
Powell (01179 732431)
Polished concrete Shortman
(01454 329283)
Honeycomb aluminium panels

Resurgem (01179 372846)
Sanitaryware Duravit
(0845 500 7787)
Shower and taps Tapstore.com
(0843 658 0062)
Kitchen units IKEA (ikea.com)
Kitchen worktop Corian
(dupont.co.uk)
Woodburning stove Stûv
(stuv.com)
Wood-fired range (W35) Esse
(01282 813235)

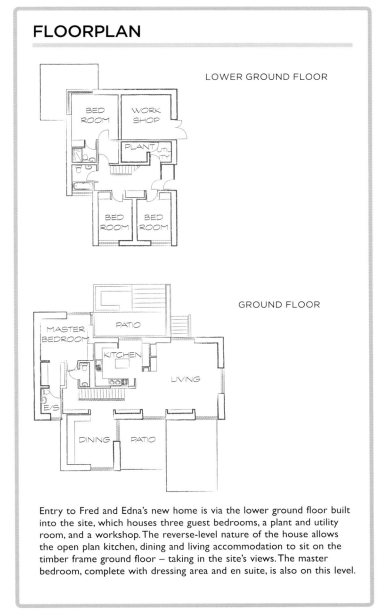

FLOORPLAN

LOWER GROUND FLOOR

GROUND FLOOR

Entry to Fred and Edna's new home is via the lower ground floor built into the site, which houses three guest bedrooms, a plant and utility room, and a workshop. The reverse-level nature of the house allows the open plan kitchen, dining and living accommodation to sit on the timber frame ground floor – taking in the site's views. The master bedroom, complete with dressing area and en suite, is also on this level.

"From the nature of the site to the innovative nature of the design, it has been far from straightforward. But we've ended up with a wonderful house that is a pleasure to live in"

Mid-Century Modernised

Neil and Anita Turner saw the potential (and beauty) in a Sixties house – turning it into an astonishing home that serves as a great example of what can be done with even the most unfashionable of styles

WORDS: JASON ORME
PHOTOGRAPHY: JEREMY PHILLIPS

The Sixties house had been altered and extended in the preceding decades, with a blocky side extension being the significant problem, along with a roof that hid the original clerestory windows

With the side wing completed, construction of the basement garage began.

A new staircase allows light to penetrate the hallway. Large windows on the north-facing elevation add to the enjoyment of the cosy library space (left).

The five magnificent poles — two have been added to the original three — are clad in iroko

There was no way we would have been able to get hold of the house if it hadn't been so unfashionable," says Anita Turner of the property that, after a short but intensive injection of excellent design and not inconsiderable vision, is now home to her and husband Neil. "We had previously been second out of 12 bidders on a period farmhouse and were more than ready to move from our Edwardian home," she continues. "When we saw the estate agent's details for this, it looked pretty unappealing. But when we saw it, we knew what it could become."

The 1964 property had been extended once before with a small granny flat added a couple of years after the house was built, and a more comprehensive extension and alteration scheme came in the early 1990s, creating a blocky two storey structure to the side of the original and introducing an unusual roof arrangement. "The original house was actually really lovely," says Neil, an architect. "The existing cantilevered balcony had railings and metal columns added to support the roof. The extended property lacked any charm and style but we could see that, using the inspiration of the original design, we could combine everything into one unique, modern family home."

It was, to a large extent, the site that sold it to the couple. An astonishingly peaceful and quite rectangular 1.7 acres, sloping down quite heavily from the rear to a private road, and scattered with and surrounded by towering pines and firs. It even came with its own river at the foot. The majority of the land is to the front but, as the road only serves a few other houses, it is the epitome of privacy and tranquillity.

Drawing inspiration from the Sixties original was key to Neil and Anita's plan – in a way trying to strip back the later additions and recapture that true essence. First of all this involved recreating the original dual monopitch roof, including revealing the original

The double-height kitchen makes use of the newly built right-hand part of the house, with the original kitchen now used as a link dining space and snug. The window frames line up exactly with the poles

One of the children's bedrooms overlooks the kitchen. A NIBE ground-source heat pump powers the underfloor heating

Occupying part of the newly constructed right-hand part of the house, a children's bedroom enjoys views to three aspects

clerestory windows (which can now be opened to provide some handy natural stack ventilation) on the first floor landing that had been boarded over. Ripping off the roof enabled the house to integrate the blockier side extension. But in a way, the success of this project is as much about what Neil and Anita have kept, and emphasised, rather than what they have taken away. For instance, the large (zinc-covered) roof overhang has been used to provide shelter on the front south elevation from the sun (more on which later) and, best of all, the original pillars have been added to (from three to five) and clad, quite beautifully, in iroko.

A site like this really does deserve its priority in design terms and so a new two storey structure, added to the right-hand (eastern) side of the elevation enjoys large windows – the kitchen is now a double-height space which just cries 'wow', while the new bedroom gets light thanks to a clever internal window. Externally, the opening elements of the bespoke window arrangement are actually cedar clad – they work a bit like stable doors – allowing the windows to remain fixed. "It helps with a feeling of security and suits the house perfectly," says Anita. Elsewhere, an external rendered wall insulation system from Sto mixes with a healthy dose of T-jointed cedar cladding. The original Sixties block and brick-built house had enjoyed a limited element of cavity wall insulation over the years – "we insulated the cavity properly, and then added 135mm of EPS (expanded polystyrene) insulation as part of the Sto system," says Neil. "The result is walls that are off the scale in terms of performance and less than 0.1 U values." (See page 58). Suffice to say heating the house is not a problem.

The practice that Neil works for runs a varied set of projects from residential to large-scale commercial schemes, and so in addition to the design, he was able to bring considerable experience of managing complicated schemes to the table. "I broke down the project into 147 work packages, all designed in detail and pretty much fully specified. The packages would be things like masonry for the new work, roof structure and so on. We then got a main contractor to price them all up and come up with a very detailed fixed price for the job. In a way it's a risky approach because if you're not too experienced in construction there might be things you forget, and small creep across lots of packages doesn't seem a lot at the time but obviously quickly adds up. However, it did help us to manage costs – if one package went over, we could always reduce down another one. The main contractor worked on an agreed cost plus basis."

The result is quite something. The best of the original Sixties design has been brought out, with sloping internal ceilings, those funky clerestory windows, and pillars to boot. The double-height kitchen dining space is brilliantly architectural; the adjacent living room has benefitted by more simple changes (the heightening of a ceiling – the levels were very complex – and the widening of a window opening). In many ways this is a modernist restoration project as much as a remodel – and all the better for it. Rooms are generous in size without becoming impersonal, and extra touches like the impressive lighting scheme and the architect's eye for detail (Neil reckons he drew around 120 details to make sure things worked, like the window frame lining up with the pillar) turn it into the perfect mix of high design and a warm, soulful family home.

"We've really pushed it in terms of scale of project and cost," says Anita (the couple spent around £300,000, which has been more than worth it – not that they ever intend to leave). "The house had been on the market for months and it was its undesirability that got us to where we are now and we would never have got it otherwise. These unfashionable mid-century houses can be such amazing modern homes – all they need is a bit of vision. Even better, shortly after we had moved in, the son of the original architect knocked on the door and said how proud his father would have been of the work completed. You can't get a better compliment than that."

FACT FILE

Name: Neil and Anita Turner
Area: Northumberland
Build type: Remodel and extension
Size: 256m²

Build date: Feb–2013
House cost: £625,000
Build cost: £300,000
Cost/m²: £1,171
House value: £1.25m

CONTACTS

Architect Neil Turner at Howarth Litchfield Partnership (0191 384 9470)
Timber columns, specialist joinery and staircase steps Swandene (0191 419 7320)
Mechanical work H Malone & Sons Ltd (0191 285 1176)
Electrical work R Lightfoot (01388 663116)
Render Sto (01418 928000)
Roof VMZinc (01992 822288)
Windows Hadrian Group (0191 414 8090)
Timber panels to windows West End Cabinet & Joinery Ltd (0191 414 4469)
Kitchen Mowlem and Co (0191 257 6112)
Sanitaryware PT Ranson

(0191 469 6999)
Slate flooring The Natural Slate Company (020 8371 1485)
Timber flooring Havwoods (01524 737000)
Staircase Architectural Metalworkers Ltd (0191 418 7222)
External lighting Marl international (01229 582430)
Internal lighting Flos (flos.com)
Blinds Jeffrey Carr of Team Valley (0191 487 3249)
Ground-source heat pump NIBE (0845 095 1200)
Photovoltaic panels WeRSolarUK (0800 211 8090)

FLOORPLAN

GROUND FLOOR

FIRST FLOOR

The ground floor benefits from a large open plan kitchen diner with a separate living room, library and snug accessed off the main hall. A utility and lobby run off the kitchen with access to a staircase leading down to the basement garage (not shown here). While there is a bedroom and bathroom at ground level, further bedroom accommodation can be found on the first floor – two with en suites. Another bathroom and a study can also be found on the first floor.

New Wave

First-time self-builders Gareth and Lisa
Maxwell have built a cutting-edge eco home

WORDS: JASON ORME PHOTOGRAPHY: SIMON MAXWELL

The new house, built out of steel frame and clad in a mix of natural stone and timber, draws on the traditional simple barn form. Owners Martin and Kelly bought an old bungalow that had been advertised as "for refurbishment", but decided to replace it – in a different location with better orientation on the valley site

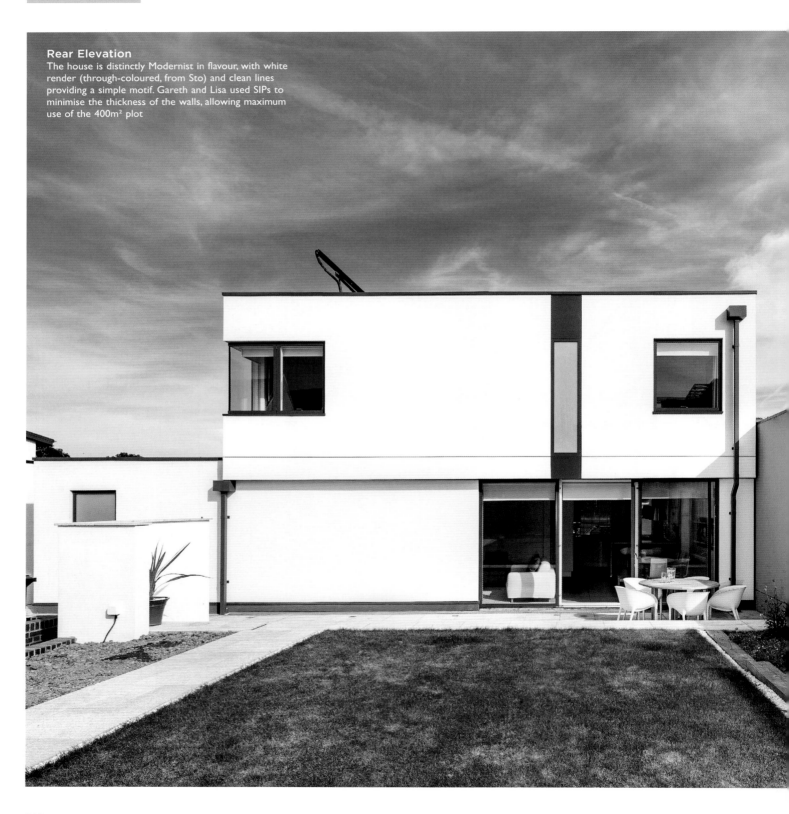

Rear Elevation
The house is distinctly Modernist in flavour, with white render (through-coloured, from Sto) and clean lines providing a simple motif. Gareth and Lisa used SIPs to minimise the thickness of the walls, allowing maximum use of the 400m² plot

The Site
The plot sits in Newhall, Harlow, which is probably the UK's most architecturally aware housing development. Leading architects have been employed to develop new housing schemes, and many individual plots have been sold off to self-builders like Gareth and Lisa

Gareth and Lisa Maxwell's project in Essex is one of the first examples of how self-build in the UK might shape up, if the plans for large-scale serviced plots get off the ground. Everything about the way they have built this house – their first as a young family – is cutting edge, from the plot-buying process to its design to, finally, its method of construction.

"I'd always wanted to build our own home," says Gareth, a design engineer in the automotive industry, while Lisa, a management consultant, agreeing that "it would be great to do," happily admits that Gareth was the (very wise, as it turns out) driving force behind the idea initially. "We looked for plots for three years, on and off," says Gareth, "and then we got to hear about this."

The site that Gareth and Lisa chose for their new home was part of the Newhall Projects estate which, thanks to the wishes of the farmer who agreed the sale of the land to the developers in the first instance, is unlike any other housing estate – in fact, those very words don't really seem to do the place justice. It is the only housing development in the UK to have a strong architectural agenda (the developers invited architects including Richard Murphy to design for it) and, as part of the ethos of the project, a small number of plots were given over to self-builders and advertised on the open market. Which is where Gareth and Lisa found it. "The view is what sold the plot of land to us," says Lisa. "I work in the City and have a very hectic day but I love coming back here to our roof terrace and sitting outside on a nice summer's evening."

"The 400m² (about 1/10 of an acre) plot cost £145,000 with gas, electricity, water and drainage already put in," explains Gareth. "There were surprisingly few constraints in terms of how the house was to look, just some guidelines on material usage and the ridge

Living Space

The open plan ground floor layout makes the most of the house's fairly modest footprint, combining a kitchen (from Tecnocucina), dining and living space. The pendant lights are from Flos and the art is from local artist Jean Noble

Corner windows help provide plenty of light in the master bedroom

height, as well as it achieving a minimum of Level 3 of the Code for Sustainable Homes. As part of the contract, we would also have to use a RIBA-registered architect."

Enter Richard Dudzicki, the talented London-based architect whose own home in East Dulwich was featured in *Homebuilding & Renovating* back in 2009. "We saw the article and thought, this is someone we can work with," says Gareth. "We wanted something very sustainable, energy and space efficient (given the constraints of the plot) and, importantly, something modern. A light, open plan living space was essential."

Which brought them on to the use of Kingspan TEK – which Richard has used before – a leading SIPs (structural insulated panels) system. Not only do SIPs walls make it easier to achieve low U-values and high levels of airtightness, but they can do so on relatively thin wall thicknesses, meaning that on tight plots such as

Gareth and Lisa's, where every inch counts, they can help create bigger interior spaces.

This is in many ways a model eco home. It actually achieves Level 4 of the Code for Sustainable Homes, meets the Lifetime Homes Standard (which promotes flexibility of design for future needs) and features solar thermal panels and underfloor heating, as well as a 'wind catcher', which is a very effective form of natural ventilation.

As Building Regulations require homes to be both better insulated and more airtight, and introducing passive solar gain as a heating method gains more widespread take-up, one of the bigger issues facing homeowners is how to keep their new homes cool and ventilated.

While mechanical ventilation systems do the job adequately, it is also possible to introduce 'designed' natural ventilation into

Roof Terrace
Accessed from the first-floor bedrooms, the decked roof terrace enjoys views over the fields to the front of the plot. The flat roof system is from Alumasc

"A lot of the value in the building has come about due to good architecture. When we have guests stay, they comment that the light quality here is so much better than their own houses. It really makes a difference"

the structure to maintain air flow. The Windcatcher system that Gareth and Lisa used is one such form of passive stack system. It works by being divided internally into quadrants, so that one or more face into the wind, and relies on the basic principle of warm air rising. The windward quadrants supply fresh air, and leeward quadrants extract stale air under the action of negative wind pressure.

The whole system uses dampers which can be controlled by the homeowner to regulate cooling, and it uses no energy at all. It looks a bit like a large flue on the outside of the house, and inside you'll see a vent measuring around 600mm². The whole thing costs around £600.

For first-time self-builders, this is an ambitious project using some sophisticated building technologies, such as I-beams for the first floor structure, pocket doors, shadow gaps and glulam beams. For all its innovation, however, it's almost slightly comforting to know that some familiar problems – in this case, builder-shaped – could not be ironed out. "That was a low point," says Gareth. "About three months into the build, we had problems with one of the builders and had to pick up the pieces. Throughout that whole period we weren't watertight, which became very difficult. Once we got the new builder on board things became rosier."

The success of this project is not just the fact that it happened at all, but that it happened so well. Most first-time self-builders would be glad to have got through the process unscathed and be ready to move on to the next, lessons learned and ready to be put into practice. But Gareth and Lisa's careful planning and methodical approach to the brief and specification of this house has resulted in a well-designed, liveable, stylish modern home that has impeccable eco credentials and is delightfully efficient in terms of its impact.

It's also of a scale that can be achieved by many people, and is a perfect example of why, rather than grand spaces or megabuck budgets, it is in fact good design that makes self-build such a satisfying route to getting your own home.

FLOORPLAN

GROUND FLOOR

FIRST FLOOR

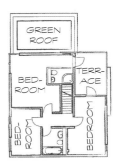

A large proportion of the ground floor is given over to an open plan kitchen, dining and living space, but there's also a study which can double as an additional bedroom when required. Upstairs are three double bedrooms, two of which lead on to a roof terrace.

FACT FILE

Name: Gareth and Lisa Maxwell
Area: Essex
Build type: Eco-home self-build
Size: 174m²
Build date: July 2009–May 10

Land cost: £145,000
Build cost: £225,000
Cost/m²: £1,293
Total cost: £370,000
House value: £500,000

CONTACTS

Architect Richard Dudzicki Associates (020 8299 2222)
SIPs Kingspan TEK (01544 388601)
Flat roof Alumasc (01536 383844)
Boiler Keston (01482 443005)
Finance BuildStore (0845 223 4888)

Kitchen Tecnocucina (tecnocucina.com)
Warranty Premier Guarantee (0844 412 0888)
Windcatcher Monodraught (monodraught.com)
Windows Velfac (01223 897100)
Render Sto (sto.co.uk)

Front Elevation
The new house is built on the site of a former sawmill, which itself replaced a tuberculosis sanitorium. An open-loop ground-source heat pump sits in the new lake to the front of the house. The garage doors are from Hörmann; the stone is from the local Veizey's Quarry

Carved from stone

Richard and Catriona Tyson's new oak frame
home in Gloucestershire is a masterclass in
the contemporary use of natural materials

WORDS: JASON ORME AND DEBBIE JEFFERY PHOTOGRAPHY: SIMON MAXWELL

Natural But Modern

The brilliant curved front elevation appears to be built in dry stone walling – in fact, this is illusory, as the mortar has simply been hidden. Throughout the interiors, partition walls, where they do exist, tend to be less than full height in order to allow light to flow through. Wedi backing board was used for the showers to prevent the plasterboard getting damp. The freestanding bath is from Fired Earth

It's no wonder, really, that a site with such an interesting history and bucolic landscape has now become host to a home that mixes the most futuristic of architectural forms with a feel that – thanks to its use of local materials – looks to the past. "Our children had left home and we wanted to live in an oak frame building," explains Catriona Tyson who, along with husband Richard, bought the sawmill and large woodland site with a view to creating a new home. "We also knew that we wanted to live in one space and use all of it. We were living in an old vicarage at the time which was very dark, so light was also very important to us when designing a new home."

The site had once been occupied by the sanitorium that was home to the tuberculosis-laden George Orwell during his final days (he actually died at University College Hospital in London) and, after the building was demolished, became a sawmill with a modest "shed" (as

Catriona calls it) which had permission for a small, three bedroom bungalow replacement. Having initially approached the company they had long desired to build the frame, Carpenter Oak & Woodland, Catriona and Richard, in turn, found George Batterham at Batterham Matthews Design Ltd to design the overall scheme – based on an open plan layout, with exposed oak framing.

"The clients had a really clear vision for how they wanted to live," says George. "They wanted to build a home that not only responded to the spectacular 200 acre woodland setting, but offered sustainable, eco friendly living." The contemporary, concave design of the home mirrors the dewdrop-shaped lake built to the front of the property. "The curved design came about early on in the planning process," explains George.

With planning permission being relatively straightforward – as the planning department were keen to encourage a thoughtful design –

work could commence on site, with a concrete floor slab specified to minimise sound travelling around the finished interiors.

"Despite the abundance of timber on site, we ended up importing the oak from France," says Catriona. "The oak over there is much straighter and therefore better for construction. The team from Carpenter Oak & Woodland erected the whole thing on site in five days." A blockwork basement and external walls, marvellously clad in local stone that has been given a hidden mortar to replicate a kind of contemporary dry stone wall, makes for an interesting variety of materials on site. The finished roof is a mix of sedum and lead. "It was all on time and on budget," Catriona explains of the construction of the house itself.

The most significant barriers to happy homebuilding were not planners or builders however, but a raft of conditions that held up progress – particularly those relating to wildlife. "We had the misfortune of having to have a bat survey," says Catriona, "which resulted in the most protracted process. Many months later, we ended up having to erect what I call the 'bat palace' [HB&R had a private tour of it and it's basically a small bungalow with four separate 'rooms' for the different types of bat the site seems to attract. Suffice to say that, since its erection, not a single bat has patronised it.] We also had to have a snail survey, which led to some mild amusement for the builders who had to enjoy/endure an education session from a local wildlife welfare officer on what to do if they happened to come across an escargot."

Slightly unusual diversions aside, this project is a huge success, not least for its exceptional eco credentials. Renewables are in abundance here, with the property featuring solar thermal and photovoltaic (PV) panels, an open-loop ground-source heat pump which feeds through a borehole and runs through the lake at the front of the house, woodburning stoves and a rainwater harvester. A heavy dose of Rockwool insulation has also been used, and the new home has now

achieved Level 4 of the Code for Sustainable Homes. "Richard and Catriona were strongly in support of the home being as sustainable as possible," explains George. "The only thing we didn't include was a mechanical ventilation heat recovery system – had we done this, the house would have achieved Level 5."

The resulting home is an impressive achievement. The monolithic, curved front elevation, hiding minimal windows with all but an imposing entrance area on show, is softened considerably by the stone. Despite this, it's inside that the design really makes itself obvious – with a charming curved open plan layout that is the main living space, including kitchen, eating and sitting zones. "We even curved the oak in the frame to enhance the gentle feel," says Catriona. An office and bedroom sit separately on this ground floor level, but thanks to the clever use of internal glass and half-height walling, the flow is maintained. Even more unusually – thanks possibly to nothing more knowing than their excellent design eye – Richard and Catriona's charming Arts & Crafts furniture sits in the space perfectly – in most cases, 'old' furniture just doesn't suit these kind of interiors. The whole effect is organic, earthy, and even reminiscent of architect Frank Lloyd Wright's work.

After three years – from first developing ideas for a home on this site to the house's completion – the result is a truly magnificent oak frame dwelling that sits perfectly within its surroundings. "There is nothing fiddly or complicated about the home. It is a stunningly bold, simple and yet carefully detailed, curved home that the owners can be proud of and enjoy – and we absolutely love it too!" concludes George.

Building in oak frame

"Our team were on site for about five days," recalls Tim Burrell, MD of Carpenter Oak & Woodland, who designed and built the curved oak frame in collaboration with George Batterham Design Ltd. "But, our involvement really began at the conceptual stage. Oak frames are either after-thoughts to the design scheme – as in the house is designed and then the owners/architects decide they want to have some oak – or they are a fundamental part of the scheme, as in this case," he says. "As a result of this approach, the oak frame design almost comes first.

"Richard and Catriona approached us first, and we put them in touch with George. It is vital for us that the architect coming up with the overall scheme has a total understanding of working with oak frames, and George is one of the best in the country at doing so. It makes everything so much smoother.

"In the case of Richard and Catriona's house, the oak frame is a genuine skeletal form, with the structure holding everything together," he continues. "In a way, that's probably why it's seen as so successful. This isn't a hybrid system using structural insulated panels – the oak frame is a skeleton, off which the external walls tie in. Achieving modern energy-efficiency standards is just a factor of the amount of insulation and wall finishes specified. Oak frames work most efficiently on a grid pattern, but there's nothing to say that the frame can't be curved slightly," he continues. "The curves are actually slightly faceted, but it all helps to work with the site and the look the architect and client were aiming for. The key is to curve the wallplates. The oak was mainly from France, which is usually straighter and is therefore better for the construction."

FLOORPLAN

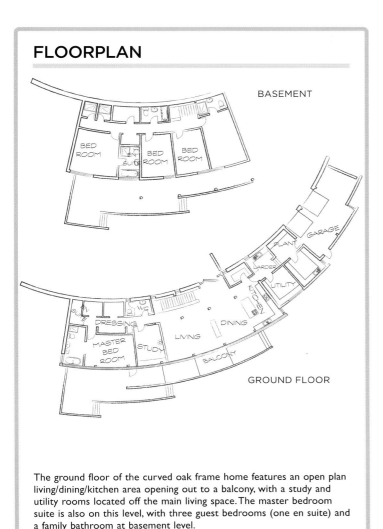

BASEMENT

GROUND FLOOR

The ground floor of the curved oak frame home features an open plan living/dining/kitchen area opening out to a balcony, with a study and utility rooms located off the main living space. The master bedroom suite is also on this level, with three guest bedrooms (one en suite) and a family bathroom at basement level.

FACT FILE

Name: Richard and Catriona Tyson
Area: Gloucestershire
Build type: Self-build
Size: 385m²
Build date: July 2011–Aug 12

Land cost: £300,000 (part of a larger holding)
Build cost: £848,466
Cost/m²: £2,203
House value: £1,400.000

CONTACTS

Design Batterham Matthews Design Ltd (01225 851122)
Green oak frame Carpenter Oak & Woodland Ltd (01225 743089)
Main contractor, timber joinery and kitchen H B Lewis & Sons Ltd (01453 845405)
Stonework Veizey's Quarry (01666 504689)
Cavity wall insulation Rockwool Ltd (01656 862621)
Sliding windows and doors Clearway (01242 513322)
Rooflights Standard Patent Glazing (01924 461213)
Garage doors Hörmann (01530 513000)
Frameless glass Roman Glass (01453 752455)
Landscape and lake TE Gifford Landscapes (07884 258698)
Sedum roof Weatherguard (0800 747 1158)
Flooring The Solid Wood Flooring Company (01666 504015)
Internal doors Premdor

(0844 209 0008)
Bathroom floor tiles Mandarin Stone (01242 530500)
Kitchen tiles The Winchester Tile Company (01392 473005)
Ceramic white tiles Ceramic Tile Trading (01454 310122)
Timber decking and cladding Vastern Timber Co (0800 135 7023)
Woodburner supply R W Knight & Son (01225 891469)
Scan DSA Woodburner Scan (01527 506019)
Heat pump Soleco 24 3 phase heat pump (0845 095 3300)
Borehole Geotechnical Engineering Ltd (01452 527743)
Solar PV panels Ecovision Systems Ltd (01666 501580)
Groundworks Laverty Construction (07837 408928)
Bathrooms Alternative Bathrooms (0203 375 9009)
Stepoc concrete retaining walls Anderton Concrete Product (01606 535300)
Consulting engineers Momentum (01225 444194)

"We wanted to live in an oak frame building. We also knew that we wanted to live in one space and use all of it"

Living off the Land

Nestled into the landscape of their 300-acre farm, Neil and Mary Gourlay's self-built home is the ultimate in sustainable living

WORDS: CAROLINE EDNIE
PHOTOGRAPHY: ANDREW LEE

The brief was for a new home that would have as little impact upon the surrounding landscape as possible. This has been successfully achieved thanks to the use of materials such as stone and timber, sourced from the surrounding land, along with a sloping turf roof which matches the gradient of the slope into which the house is built

LIVING OFF THE LAND

The exterior of the property features a mix of materials sourced from the surrounding farmland. The majority of the home's façade is clad in oak from the site's wind-felled trees, while 500 tonnes of stone was collected from the neighbouring fields to create the dry-stone wall. The turf roof also uses grass from the site

hen Neil Gourlay set out to project manage his first major self-build, the experience saw the Dumfries and Galloway farmer extend his portfolio beyond the accolade of the UK's 'green energy farmer of the year (2011)' to becoming one of Britain's greenest self-builders.

What has emerged following Neil and wife Mary's 'four Rs' philosophy – reduce, reuse, recycle and recover – is Three Glens, a new long-term family home set among farmland, which is also something of a masterstroke of eco-savvy design and technology.

"Our solution wasn't to build an ordinary house," explains Neil of the couple's off-grid home, located on a 300-acre farm site which they bought back in 2002, and adjoins the Gourlays' substantial, mainly grass farmland, which is also home to 3,200 ewes and 500 cows.

The catalyst for building what is essentially their 'retirement' home – they are the third generation of the Gourlay family farming in the Cairn Valley – was actually the recent financial crisis. "I decided to take the family funds and put them back into my own hands, and do something that I had control over. My options were to do something with the land or on the land, and it was at this point that we decided to build," explains Neil.

Essentially, when it came to finding their self-build plot, there were 300 acres of farmland for the couple to choose from. "It was easy enough getting planning permission to build a house for agricultural use, in order to ensure the security and wellbeing of the livestock and make sure there was someone there keeping an eye on the land," explains Neil.

The specific site eventually chosen for the build was based on a decision reached by the Gourlays in conjunction with their architect, Mark Waghorn, who was responsible for the design of Three Glens. "When we first spoke to Mark, our main brief was for a long-term family home that would be sustainable and carbon negative, warm and airtight, and that would not cost a lot in terms of power and heating," Neil continues. "Already, we have no telephone or internet bills (we don't have a landline), nor heating, electricity or gas bills, as a wind turbine services the house. All we've got to pay is the council tax and by the time we're 65, we won't even be paying for our TV licence!

"We were also keen that the house would incorporate as

The ground-floor living space is open plan, with a feature dry-stone wall. Large triple-glazed windows offer majestic views of the surrounding farmland

The feature dry-stone wall houses a Kachelöfen Austrian biomass stove

many materials from the farmland as possible and blend into the landscape," says Neil. "In the event, Mark chose a site where solar gains would be enjoyed yet at the same time where the house's visual impact on the landscape would be minimal (a copse of trees and outcrop of rocks naturally frames the building). The final design also has a roof slope that has the same gradient as the slope of the hill – it has a view to die for!"

The substantial five bedroom farmhouse finally emerged in 2013 following a 17-month build by 3b Construction, with the whole project managed by Neil himself. "Our main concern during the build was that water from the hillside would penetrate the property, so we started with a poured concrete wall and then a steel frame; it had to be a steel frame to take the weight of the turf roof. We took the turf from the site and, as well as being visually

attractive, it also keeps the sun off the Sarnafil flat roof and protects it from any deterioration."

In order to stay true to their 'four Rs' philosophy, Three Glens embraces the land from which it is quite literally built. Alongside the use of self-grown turf for the roof, the exterior oak cladding was sourced from the surrounding wind-felled trees, while 500 tonnes of stone from neighbouring fields have been used for the dry-stone wall which passes through the interior of the house. If that wasn't enough, the couple have even used homegrown sheep fleece to insulate the property.

"We clipped the sheep about four years ago and I took all the fleeces down to Bradford and had them scoured – there are only two wool scourers left in the country now," explains Neil. "The wool went from there to a company down the road, John Cotton,

A staircase in the centre of the ground-floor living area leads down to the bedrooms

which made it into batts. I took the wool fleeces down in my pick-up truck and it took two arctic lorries to bring it back; not from weight but bulk. There's now 150mm of sheep's wool insulation behind every wall."

Along with heavy doses of insulation, the property benefits from a plethora of energy-efficient solutions, including a Kachelöfen biomass stove, which sits at the heart of the house and warms up the interior dry-stone wall, evenly distributing the heat to create a constant ambient temperature. A ground-source heat pump (dug vertically to a depth of 100m) is also in place to power the underfloor heating, and a mechanical ventilation heat recovery system ups the ante in terms of energy self-sufficiency. A 34m-tall wind turbine also generates enough electricity for up to 25 homes, with the excess electricity exported to the National Grid and generating extra income for the farm.

The only disappointment for Neil in terms of the kit installed has been the solar thermal panels on the garage roof, "which haven't

performed as well as the other systems, although I'm not blaming the equipment, just the weather!"

The 'reduce, reuse, recycle, recover' build philosophy is also largely evident in the interiors, where reclaimed railway sleepers have been sawn, treated and polished by local craftspeople to create the wood floors and functional furniture; leather hide from the farm's cows has even been used for the upholstery, too.

"The advantage of project managing every aspect is that your research is done beforehand and you think about details and interesting features before taking on the build," says Neil. "For example, the round clock in the living area was made on my father-in-law's farm in Cumbria, using his mill wheel stone. I made sure that it was incorporated and built into the design – you can't do these kind of things retrospectively.

"Ultimately taking on a project like this, in addition to the 'four Rs', is also about the six Ps!" laughs Neil, looking back. "That's 'proper preparation prevents piss-poor performance'!"

FLOORPLAN

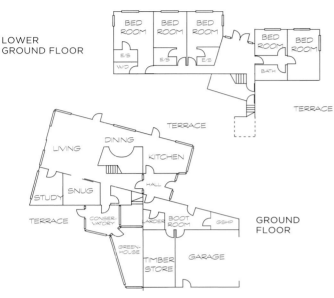

LOWER GROUND FLOOR

BED ROOM
BED ROOM
BED ROOM
BED ROOM
BED ROOM
E/S
W/D
E/S
E/S
BATH
TERRACE

TERRACE

LIVING
DINING
KITCHEN

STUDY
SNUG
HALL

TERRACE
CONSER-VATORY
LARDER
BOOT ROOM
GSHP
GROUND FLOOR

GREEN-HOUSE
TIMBER STORE
GARAGE

With the brief for the home to have as little impact on the landscape as possible, the house is built into the hill slope with the living accommodation at ground level, and five bedrooms below. In order to maximise on the surrounding views, two large terraces lead out from the open plan living/kitchen/dining space, while a third terrace is accessed from the conservatory. A separate snug and study offer more private spaces to retreat to. To the front of the house, a section is dedicated to utility areas including a larder, timber store, double garage and a space to house the ground-source heat pump.

FACT FILE

Name: Neil and Mary Gourlay
Area: Dumfries and Galloway
Build type: Eco self-builld
Size: 340m²
Build date: Dec 2011–Jan 13

Land cost: £0 (already owned)
Build cost: £700,000
Cost/m²: £2,058
House value: £800,000

CONTACTS

Architect Mark Waghorn Architects (markwaghorn.co.uk)
Structural engineer, main contractor, stone finishes, plumbing and heating 3b Construction (3bconstruction.co.uk)
Concrete supplier Hansons (hansonready-mixconcrete.co.uk)
Windows Ling Joinery

(01931 714289)
Sanitaryware Tynemouth Architectural Salvage (01912 966070)
Kitchen and appliances Stevenson McConnel (01387 740112)
Fleece scouring John Cotton (01924 496571)

Secret weapon: the biomass stove

"The Austrian stove is wonderful," says Neil, who first came across the Kachelöfen stove while on holiday in the country. "I thought at the time, 'This has to be the way to heat a house.' It only takes about four logs a day to heat it; you bung the logs in and keep the air vent open so the oxygen is there to burn it down to the ashes, and then you switch off the oxygen and that's all it takes, until the next day.

"It could be described as a solid-mass pizza oven," he explains. "A pizza oven is open, but when this fires up you close the door and it heats the whole oven up. It's made from lime mortar rather than cement, which means that it can contract and expand without cracking.

"It heats up the whole dry-stone wall that runs through the house. As it's located in the wall between the main living space, an element goes into the snug room and an element goes into the study, heating all these areas. And it evenly distributes the heat, so you don't have warm and cold areas. The biggest complaints from guests are that the house is too hot, even on this exposed site."

Boxing Clever

The planners wouldn't allow Ian and Lucy to replace their
Fifties house with a contemporary home. So, with the help
of architect Dan Brill, they did something even better...

WORDS: JUDE WEBLEY   PHOTOGRAPHY: NIGEL RIGDEN

> "Normally, planning constraints compromise a project. In this case I think we were able to be quite clever and use them to our advantage"

Living Area & Kitchen

The first floor contains a cosier living room, which doubles as a playroom and study. Lucy is a keen cook, so the kitchen was at the heart of her plans and, therefore, the meeting point for the house. There's a pantry next to the built-in oven to take the strain of the storage, allowing the clean contemporary lines to work uncluttered. The kitchen is from Callerton

BOXING CLEVER

In architecture as in life, sometimes the cleverest solutions, the ones that really appear to push the boundaries forward, are those borne out of the simplest approaches. This is undoubtedly true of the astonishing remodel and extension project undertaken by Ian and Lucy who, with the help of talented architect Dan Brill, have transformed their Fifties detached home into a quite remarkable contemporary-style family home.

"We were renting just down the road, and loved the area so much we wanted to stay here," says Lucy, who is, along with husband Ian, a schoolteacher. "We always wanted to do a new build and when this house came available, we went after it." Architect Dan Brill, who they appointed upon the recommendation of friends, takes up the story. "The planners, however, wanted us to keep what was, frankly, a quite banal post-war home because it was in keeping with all the other houses in the neighbourhood," he explains. But far

Master Bedroom
Birch-faced ply and a polished concrete floor provide a contemporary feel in the master en suite bedroom, which connects to the garden through sliding doors

The Extension
The steel and timber-framed extension is clad in cedar, treated with three coats of UV-protecting oil (Osmo are the leading supplier). All of the bedrooms open out onto the courtyard-style garden

"We kept the minimum that was needed to satisfy the planners and all the rest was unashamedly modern to meet Ian and Lucy's brief"

Living Space
The internal walls of the original house have been completely removed, as has half of the first floor structure, to allow for a dramatic double-height living, eating and kitchen space. The fireplace is built out of in-situ concrete; the woodburning stove is from Stûv

from giving up on the dream of a stunning contemporary home, Dan realised that the couple's goal was still achievable.

"It was the planning constraints that gave rise to the concept," says Dan. "Normally planning constraints compromise a project. In this case I think we were able to be quite clever and use them to our advantage. The conceptual approach was to treat the existing house as a veil or stage set which keeps the façade to the street but nothing more. We kept the minimum that was needed to satisfy the planners and all the rest was unashamedly modern to meet Ian and Lucy's brief, which was to provide a large open plan living area and series of bedrooms. The only way we could do that was to turn the existing house into the open plan living area – involving gutting all the small rooms that were there – to create a single large space. The question then was where to put the bedrooms. The concept of a long box that skewers through the house was quite a good solution. It allowed us to provide a line of bedrooms all linked by a corridor. It was quite a radical idea but one that has worked out really well."

Radical is certainly one way to describe it. The existing house, with almost all internal walls and most of the first floor structure ripped out, has become a dramatic double-height open plan living space. The fact that the existing window openings have been maintained only adds to the conceit from the front elevation, where all that appears to have changed is the addition of a modern-looking, boxy porch. Yet this is in fact only the front end of the long, single storey dissecting extension structure, which accommodates four bedrooms all served by a corridor on one side, and all opening onto the garden on the other. It really is quite remarkable and easily one of the most imaginative, thoughtful and radical reworkings of an existing house ever seen in the UK.

Taking the bulk of the first floor structure out of a two storey property leaves the flank (side) walls quite structurally precarious. As a result, Ian and Lucy had to strengthen it with the addition of a windpost, which is a (usually steel) vertical support built into the wall structure to provide lateral bracing and stop the wall bowing. The new extension is a mixture of steel (Dan describes the steel frame as a bit like a 'goalpost') and timber frame, packed with hemp insulation – specified because, in Dan's words, "it's cheaper than sheeps wool and nicer to work with than mineral fibre."

Front Elevation
A boxy porch is the only sign to the outside world of the major changes that have gone on inside this Fifties house. Flush-glazed windows, from Schüco, and opening lights with aluminium frames, and the obscured front glazed panel are further modern flourishes

The Corridor
Running the whole length of the house, the corridor serves the four bedrooms. The fixed rooflights from Sunsquare provide plenty of light here, with natural ventilation through doors at either end and in the bedrooms themselves

The Staircase
The open-plan ground floor eschews the traditional entrance hall in favour of making a feature of the staircase, which is clad in birch-faced plywood. Expansion gaps in the polished concrete floor ensure future cracks are avoided

Issues with a difficult neighbour aside – which resulted in the side wall of the corridor having to be moved in a touch and highlighted the occasional failing of the Party Wall act – the rest of the project passed off fairly peacefully, with Dan and his team recognising the unusual nature of the design requiring out-of-the-ordinary levels of attention on site. "We could see as the project developed that this was going to be very special, so as a result we spent more time on site for this project than we would normally do. I think it has paid off," he says.

Too right. The lesson for those wanting to take on a radical reappraisal of an ordinary house? Be bold, and jump right in. Dan says: "Ian and Lucy were brave clients. I think people need to trust their architect. The biggest problem is that clients don't trust their architect enough and they tend to get involved too much. If they genuinely trust the architect they get the most out of them – let them do what they do best. Ian and Lucy were terrific at that. They would always ask me, 'what do you advise', and then they would take the advice. We could see that Ian and Lucy were 100 per cent behind us and trusting us all the way. Architectural projects rely on fantastic clients as well as fantastic architects."

Demolition and Planning

Ian and Lucy had significant problems with getting the planners to allow them to demolish the existing house and rebuild a contemporary home in its place. In principle the planners were not against the concept of demolition, but they reacted negatively to the contemporary nature of the proposed replacement.

In most cases, planners are happy to allow homes to be rebuilt (depending on the proposed size and design of the replacement dwelling) providing that the existing house does not have any special status (not just listed, in which case it is a criminal offence to demolish, but perhaps on a Local Heritage List, which identifies buildings that have architectural appeal).

So the lesson is not to assume that a house you are looking to knockdown and rebuild can be demolished. The argument will come down to the appeal of the existing house and, later on, the scale and design of any replacement. Within their local plans, many local authorities publish guidance on the size of 'extension' allowed when building a replacement. This varies wildly from authority to authority. Policy HS10 of the Shrewsbury & Atcham Borough Local Plan in Shropshire, for example, states that replacement dwellings must not exceed the volume of the existing plus any extra allowed under Permitted Development rights. Bear in mind, however, that size and scale are only one aspect of the consideration from a planning viewpoint – design will have a material impact too.

The conclusion? Do your research. Certainly don't demolish before you've got approval to do so, and take local expert advice on how your proposed replacement might be received by the planners.

FLOORPLAN

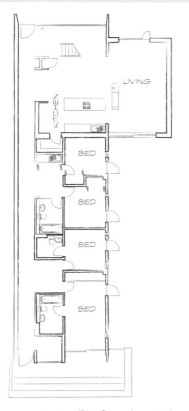

The ground-floor rear extension (first floor plan not shown) is used for the four bedrooms, all of which are accessed from the corridor, have en suites and open out onto the garden. Moving the bedrooms out of the existing two storey house allows the living space to be double height

FACT FILE

Name: Chris and Trish Sale
Profession: Architect and Housewife
Area: Hampshire
Build type: Remodel/extension
Size: 210m²

Build date: Jan–Nov 2011
House cost: £380,000
Build cost: £295,000
Total cost: £675,000
House value: £900,000
Cost/m²: £509

CONTACTS

Architect: Dan Brill Architects (01962 622085/danbrillarchitects.com)
Builder: Roger Ward (01962 884488)
Structural Engineer: Heyne Tillett (020 7870 8050)
Rooflights: Sunsquare (0845 226 3172)
Windows: Schüco (01908 282111)
Architectural Systems

Technology (023 9221 4414)
Polished concrete floor: Steyson Granolithic (020 8553 2636)
Ironmongery: Trapex (01992 462150)
Woodburning stove: Stûv (stuv.com)
Flat roof on extension: Sarnafil (01603 709360)
Kitchen: Callerton (0191 514 0003)

"Ian and Lucy were 100 per cent behind us and trusting us all the way. Architectural projects rely on fantastic clients as well as fantastic architects"

Added Style, Added Space

A Seventies bungalow is transformed thanks to a clever scheme of small extensions, external makeover and internal remodel

WORDS: JASON ORME PHOTOGRAPHY: BRETT CHARLES

The Seventies bungalow has been transformed into a contemporary home designed by whiteBOX Architects, with vertically laid stained larch, a new front door and new windows featuring. The left-hand element has been turned from a garage into usable internal space

Angie Faulker certainly had a bit of vision when she came across an individual early Seventies home on a delightful green belt riverside plot in a pretty village between Bristol and Bath. Despite its idyllic setting, the house wasn't exactly in demand – its mid-century design flourishes being somewhat lost on the 21st-century housebuying public. But in the clean lines, groovy feel and location, Angie could see the end result.

"I first met my architect Jon Foulds when I was running a smoothie bar in Bath," begins Angie. "I got to know him over the years and when I took on this house, he was the first person I went to." "Luckily," says Jon, "we shared a similar vision for the house. We could both see the potential to create a modernist-inspired home, with only modest intervention. A few tweaks externally, and a lot of internal reworking, and we knew that this could be a great house."

Seeing the potential beauty in this architectural ugly duckling, Jon (who, by this time, had set up his own practice, whiteBOX Architects) and Angie set about coming up with a scheme based on the restrictions of the 30 per cent volume increase allowed under local planning policy and the relatively modest budget of £150,000.

Fortunately, the fact that it was an existing home meant that there were no special requirements in terms of flood alleviation. Indeed, the first job was in fact to build a new self-contained 'annexe' right by the river which consists of a couple of rooms – it's little more than a poolhouse/shed – which Angie lived in while the house was deconstructed and put back together.

"Minimal intervention was key," explains Jon. "We have extended one half of the rear to create a flatter elevation, and built two new dormers (the chalet bungalow had a room in the roof but it was tiny and cramped) into the roof. We've reclad the house, added new windows and door positions, and removed and replaced plenty of the home's original internal walls. It has been completely opened up inside and it's now light, airy and really makes the most of the site." Outside, the front elevation has been reclad in vertically laid stained larch. To the rear, horizontal oak boarding provides an interesting and easily maintainable contrast to the large expanses of glazing. Stone detailing around the windows is as original, with some additional stonework added on the new gable – it looks entirely as if it has always been there. Rather than reclad the whole roof, additional concrete (round-topped) tiles were sourced from a local reclamation yard to blend back in with the ones already on the house. "It would have been nice to have slate," explains Jon, "but budget was important."

The previously pokey interior has been opened up significantly with the removal of the hallway, the separating walls and more. A sturdy steel post provides support and a useful element of zoning for the open plan ground floor. The kitchen units are from Howdens, while the work-surface is architect Jon Faulds' own design, built in walnut. The first floor-bedroom (opposite) is now very luxurious. A garden boathouse (opposite, below) was used as accommodation during building work and is now a handy annexe

Inside, the significant remodel is obvious: the extended entrance hall gives generous circulation space, which then opens up to a large, airy open plan kitchen, dining and living space, all enjoying views over the river. It's very white, very clean and very simple, with just a single orange pillar as an indication of the original layout. There are a couple of guest bedrooms and a bathroom too. Up a new solid oak staircase – purposefully narrow to ensure room to move around it in the internal hallway – the master bedroom feels light despite its low ceiling heights (one of the dormers above the staircase ensures 2m head height clearance for Building Regulations compliance). There's a clever and surprisingly generous shower in the en suite (built right into the roof space). Three rooflights in the flat roof valley (between the two gables) give plenty of light to the open plan living area too.

ADDED STYLE, ADDED SPACE

The build was run off a JCT Homeowner Contract between the main contractor and Angie, with Jon supervising at regular intervals and detailing key design elements. Inside is very much a collaboration, with Angie specifying the kitchen and most of the finishes. Extra little touches make the home special, such as the chamfered window reveals and a beautiful picture window which frames the views of the hills to the east.

"I really feel like we have pushed the house into the 21st century," continues Jon. "Actually, working with these types of houses is very nice for an architect. They have plenty of interesting forms and lots to work with – they're well-built and usually very light. It's amazing how they can be turned into something very interesting with relatively little in the way of intervention."

The new open plan ground floor enjoys a significant boost in light thanks to the south-facing glazing (above left). The windows are from Glass Consultants UK Ltd

The existing roof tiles (right) were retained, and a small extension fills the gap between the two gables of the original house. Perhaps most impressive of all are the two modern, bespoke dormers, which enable the first-floor bedroom to be much more generous in size

FACT FILE

Name: Angie Faulker
Area: Somerset
Build type: Extension and remodel
Size: 195m²

Build date: June 2012–Feb 13
House cost: £360,000
Build cost: £160,000
Cost/m²: £820
House value: £800,000

CONTACTS

Architect whiteBOX Architects Ltd (01225 314116)
Main contractor Gratton Ltd (07809 830689)
Structural engineer Franklin Associates Ltd (01225 426643)
Building Control Bath and North East Somerset Local Authority Building Control (01225 477000)
Heating engineer David Adcock Heating Services (0843 261 9082)

Rooflights Gratton Ltd (as before)
Doors and windows Glass Consultants UK Ltd (Bristol) (01179 664216)
External timber cladding and bespoke timber staircase M J Derrick (01275 839600)
Kitchen Howdens (howdens.com)
Flat roof S P Isaac (01225 339241)

FLOORPLAN

By removing and replacing the internal walls, the bungalow has now been opened up to make the most of the available space. Extending the hallway has allowed for a large circulation area with an open plan kitchen/dining/living space and separate utility and cloakroom. To the other side of the ground floor are two guest bedrooms and a bathroom. A new staircase leads to the enlarged master bedroom, which also includes an en suite.